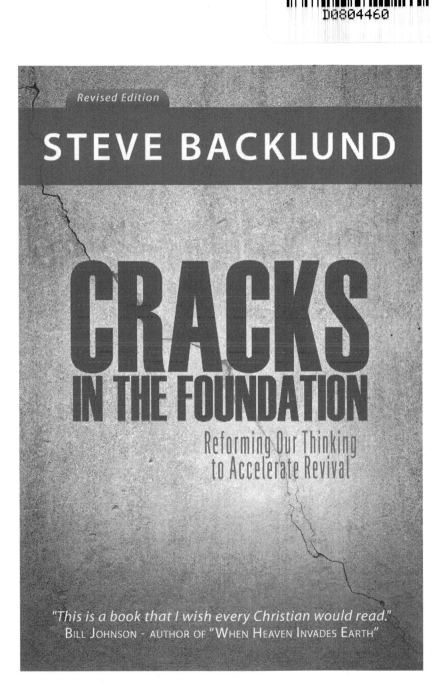

Revised Edition

STEVE BACKLUND

CRACKS
IN THE FOUNDATION
Reforming Our Thinking
to Accelerate Revival

"This is a book that I wish every Christian would read."
BILL JOHNSON - AUTHOR OF "WHEN HEAVEN INVADES EARTH"

iGNITING
HOPE
MINISTRIES

© copyright 2014 Steve Backlund, Igniting Hope Ministries
www.IgnitingHope.com

Cover Design: Linda Lee
Cover Layout/ Interior Design and Formatting: Robert Schwendenmann
Typesetting: Julie Heth
Special Assistance by: Daniel Newton, Maureen Puddle, Dan Hale
Revised Edition Editors: Julie Heth, Melissa Amato, Julie Mustard, Elizabeth Preece, Sophie Cotton

ISBN: 978-0-9863094-0-3

Please note that the author's publishing style capitalizes certain pronouns in Scripture that refer to Father, Son, and Holy Spirit and may differ from other publishers' styles.

CRACKS
IN THE FOUNDATION

TABLE OF CONTENTS

DEVOTIONALS	PAGE

PREFACE

The contents of this book are a result of my own personal journey of repairing cracks in my theological beliefs. I wrote the first edition of *Cracks in the Foundation* in 2007. Now, seven years later, I have seen some cracks needing repair in the original writing. I believe this revised version reflects even more accurately the victory Jesus won for us on the cross and through His resurrection.

Do you know what is probably going to happen? In 2021 (or sooner), I will find more cracks that will inspire another rewrite. I am continually growing in my revelation of biblical truth. So are you. As a matter of fact, if I have not significantly grown in my theological beliefs by then, I will conclude something is wrong.

When Martin Luther, in 1517 posted his 95 theses on the door of the Castle Church in Wittenburg, Germany, he started what is known as the Protestant Reformation. He saw things in the Bible which were not being taught, and he reformed the doctrinal beliefs of the global church as a result. This reformation of theological understanding continues to this day and will keep happening until this age comes to an end. Truly, the Holy Spirit will keep leading us into biblical truths we have never seen before.

Cracks in the Foundation is a book designed to help us be more open to greater revelation regarding the truths in the Bible. I am thrilled to be able to release this book with its improved content, and with added study questions and declarations which were not in the first edition. I am indebted to two members of my team, Melissa Amato and Julie Heth, for working diligently with me to upgrade this book.

I release fresh grace for revelation and blessings on your journey as the Holy Spirit leads you into all truth.

Steve Backlund

INTRODUCTION

A PARADIGM SHIFT

The term paradigm shift was originally used to describe a change in basic assumptions within the ruling theory of science. It is also used to describe a major change in a certain thought pattern – a radical change in personal beliefs or organizations. **A paradigm shift is a replacing of a former way of thinking with a radically different way of thinking.**

When I read this definition, I was struck by the phrase "a change in basic assumptions." We all have basic assumptions about God, others, the world, and ourselves. These beliefs result from our upbringing, experiences, and religious teachings, and they form a foundation for what we expect and subsequently experience in life. If we have the wrong assumptions, then we have "cracks in our foundation" that will limit what can be built in us and through us.

This is a book that challenges many basic assumptions of familiar Bible verses and other common phrases. It is designed to help you process what you believe. It has the potential to fill and repair many cracks in your thinking which rob you of your potential. You may not agree with everything written, but you will be inspired to reach a higher level in your beliefs about the key issues raised in *Cracks in the Foundation*.

Through the years, it has been wonderful to hear how this book has impacted lives. We are excited in this revised edition to have upgraded some of the content, provided questions, and given you declarations to give a greater experience for the reader.

THIS BOOK IS NOT:

- A final word on the issues addressed

THIS BOOK IS:

- A book to help you think through your belief system about key doctrinal issues
- A resource that reveals beliefs that may be a "slippery slope" for our lives

COMPONENTS OF THIS BOOK

Each chapter of the book includes six major sections. The chapter title is a phrase that is either a verse in the Bible or an implication from Scripture heard among believers.

Context
This section describes where the phrase or idea is derived from.

Positive
We look at the truth derived from the Scripture or idea that would benefit any believer.

Checking the Foundation
This section identifies the overemphasis or misinterpretation that could lead to cracks in our beliefs.

Conclusion
Considering the context, the positive, and the crack, we conclude with what we believe is the most biblical belief to have about this topic.

Discussion Questions
These are useful when using this book with a group, reading it with a friend, or to go deeper into your own beliefs.

Declarations
Speak these aloud at the end of each devotional and throughout your day as a way to begin making these truths a reality in your everyday life.

CRACKS
IN THE FOUNDATION

1 IF IT BE GOD'S WILL

CONTEXT

The words of James are directed to those who make decisions independent of God. "Come now, you who say, 'Today or tomorrow we will go to such and such a city, spend a year there, buy and sell, and make a profit;' whereas you do not know what will happen tomorrow. For what is your life? It is even a vapor that appears for a little time and then vanishes away. Instead you ought to say, 'If the Lord wills, we shall live and do this or that.' But now you boast in your arrogance. All such boasting is evil. Come, now, you who say, tomorrow we will do this or that" (James 4:13-16). This Apostle says we do not know the details of tomorrow; therefore, we should not make personal plans without a heart that says, "If it be God's will."

POSITIVE

Impulsive plans and decisions are based primarily on emotion and personal ambition, rather than God's heart. Proverbs 14:12 states, "There is a way that seems right to a man, but its end is the way of death." As we decide on choices for the future, we must always consider the big picture of our spiritual lives regarding what God is building in us.

CHECKING THE FOUNDATION

There will be a crack in our spiritual foundation if we use "if it be your will" in prayer for things God already declared as His will. 1 John 5:14,15 tells us, "Now this is the confidence that we have in Him, that if we ask anything according to His will, He hears us. And if we know that He hears us, whatever we ask, we know that we have the petitions that we have asked of Him." If we lack confidence in prayer, then we need to study God's Word until we know His promises concerning the key areas of our lives.

CONCLUDING THOUGHTS

God has called us to confidence in prayer by knowing His will about salvation, healing, provision, deliverance, etc. We don't need to pray "if it be Your will" about things clearly outlined in His Word. Yes, we need the Spirit to help us every time we pray, but we cannot doubt God's will in what was finished through Christ's death and resurrection.

DISCUSSION QUESTIONS

1. What truth stood out to you the most in this teaching?
2. How confident are you that you pray in the will of God?
3. What is one main step you can take to pray with greater confidence?

SPEAK THESE DECLARATIONS ALOUD

- I have surrendered my will to God through Jesus Christ.
- I know God's will about healing, provision, and other important areas of life.
- I pray in confidence because I know God's will.

KNOW God's PROMISES

*I JOHN 5:14 Confidence comes
(DUET. 28,31) as I KNOW God's will
by studying His word
to KNOW what HE
PROMISES concerning
our lives.*

2 ALL THINGS WORK TOGETHER FOR GOOD

CONTEXT

In Romans 8:26-27, Paul writes to the Romans about the power of "Holy Spirit praying." He ties this truth in with "all things work together for good for those who love God and are the called according to His purpose" (Romans 8:28). In verse 29, Paul speaks of the fact that we are predestined to be conformed into the image of Christ.

POSITIVE

When we turn to God with love, with praying in the Spirit, and with commitment to His call on our lives, He promises that everything in our lives will turn out for good. This includes bad things that happened to us and wrong choices we made. What a glorious promise! It may take a while for us to see all things turned to good, but God starts the process immediately once we turn our hearts to Him.

CHECKING THE FOUNDATION

There will be a crack in our spiritual foundation if we believe this verse means "all things that happen are good." Unfortunately, many believe Romans 8:28 teaches just this. This conclusion results from a misunderstanding of God's sovereignty. If we believe all circumstances are good, we will subconsciously think prayer is pointless. We will also be hindered in our ability to "resist the devil" (James 4:7) because we will never know what to resist. This may lead to not resisting sickness, addiction, or tragedy because of the belief that it could be for "our good."

Resist these things!!
SICKNESS
ADDICTION
TRAGEDY

4

CONCLUDING THOUGHTS

THIS BELIEF CAUSES PASSIVITY IN LIFE, AVOIDING TAKING RESPONSIBILITY.

Romans 8:28 is one of the greatest promises in the whole Bible. We rejoice in it because our God transforms messes into something good. That is truly good news! However, we need to be careful not to become passive and simply let life happen to us, thinking everything that happens will work out for good. This conclusion weakens our hope and makes us dependent on "I hope this works" praying, rather than being confident in prayer as God intends (1 John 5:14,15 and Mark 11:24).

DISCUSSION QUESTIONS

1. What truth stood out to you the most in this teaching?
2. Give testimonies of how negative things in your past turned positive for you.
3. Do you have a clear idea of what to resist in life and what to embrace? Explain.

SPEAK THESE DECLARATIONS ALOUD

- Every negative thing in my past is being turned to good.
- I resist the devil and he flees from me.
- I have great discernment to understand what is from God and what is from the devil.

*God's will that we stand
CONFIDENT IN
His promise to give me.
Good for the evil faced
Power to resist and evil flees
Discernment of things from God
and from devil*

5

3 HE SENDS RAIN ON THE JUST AND ON THE UNJUST

CONTEXT

This is a quote from Jesus in the Sermon on the Mount where He instructs us in our attitudes concerning our enemies, those who hate us, those who curse us, and those who persecute us (Matthew 5:44-46). As sons and daughters, we are to follow the example of our Heavenly Father in loving and in doing good to all people, even those who treat us unjustly. As we consider this, we must understand that this verse has often been taken out of context to define "rain" as negative life circumstances which seemingly happen equally to the believer and nonbeliever.

POSITIVE

Christians are called to be spiritual shock absorbers. We are called to absorb hatred and persecution in our environments through love, prayer, and forgiveness. We are to "rain" down God's goodness on those who are seemingly undeserving because God did that for us. Yes, we need boundaries in ongoing relationships, but our blessing and prayers for people who are causing difficulties will help create an open heaven for them to experience God (consider how Saul was converted in Acts 9 after he was forgiven by Stephen in Acts 7).

CHECKING THE FOUNDATION

There will be a crack in our spiritual foundation if we misinterpret this passage and think the rain (referred to here) is negative circumstances. If we conclude this, we will develop a fatalistic view of life, and we will believe there is no difference in the level of blessing between believer and nonbeliever. This perspective will create doubt in prayer and faith and will greatly hinder perseverance in waiting for God's promises to manifest.

CONCLUDING THOUGHTS

Both the believer and unbeliever face challenges in this life, but the Christian has access to divine protection from the "rain" of Satan's "killing, stealing and destroying" (John 10:10). Jesus became a curse for us so that we could be offered the "blessing of Abraham" (Galatians 3:13-14). This blessing is received by faith and increasingly manifests as we continue to abide in Him and His words continue to abide in us (John 15:7).

DISCUSSION QUESTIONS

1. What truth stood out to you the most in this teaching?
2. Do you believe there is greater blessing available for those who know God? Why or why not?
3. What are some keys for more kingdom blessings to manifest in our lives?

SPEAK THESE DECLARATIONS ALOUD

- I am increasingly walking in the blessings Jesus won for me on the cross.
- I live under a supernatural protection.
- Jesus became a curse for me so I could be blessed.

4   IT IS APPOINTED FOR MEN TO DIE ONCE

CONTEXT

Even though the writer to Hebrews is speaking of the greatness of Christ's sacrificial death for us, this verse is often used to imply that God has a preordained time for us to die – whether we are young or old, it will just be "our time." The verse actually says, "It is appointed unto men once to die, and then comes the judgment" (Hebrews 9:27). The next few verses reveal that Christ has taken our judgment and that we have the glorious expectancy of seeing God's full salvation when we die.

POSITIVE

Death is a reality that we will all face. The Bible exhorts us to be continually ready to enter into eternity. We cannot drift from God and assume that we have time to waste while doing our own thing apart from Him. The truth that "God is love" (1 John 4:8) is a great safety and inspiration to us as we look forward to spending eternity with Him.

CHECKING THE FOUNDATION

There will be a crack in our spiritual foundation if we conclude that God chooses the time for everyone to die. This thinking would be contrary to the overwhelming scriptural theme that long life is a blessing and shortened life is a curse. Believing in a preordained time to die weakens the prayer of faith for protection, and it renders beliefs and choices unimportant in affecting whether life or death is released in us and around us.

CONCLUDING THOUGHTS

We do not know all the factors that may cause a premature death in someone's life, but we need to be careful about concluding that God has chosen a time for everyone to die. In Philippians chapter 1, when Paul was struggling with whether he should live or die, he asked, "What shall I choose" (Philippians 1:22). We have more to do with our longevity on earth than we might realize. Let's press in and possess the Promised Land of long life for the church, for our descendants, and for ourselves.

DISCUSSION QUESTIONS

1. What truth stood out to you the most in this teaching?
2. Why do some people seem to believe that God has a preordained time for each person to die?
3. What are the keys for us to believe for length of days and still have great compassion for families who have had loved ones die young?

SPEAK THESE DECLARATIONS ALOUD

- I will live a long and happy life.
- My influence will continue to grow the older I become.
- I have an anointing to raise from the dead those who have died before their time.

TRUTH to BE ACTIVE not PASSIVE

LONG LIFE is a BLESSING
PROTECTION prays continually
ACCOUNTABLE for my CHOICES
POWER to RELEASE LIFE
or DEATH by passive AGREEMENT

5   GOD IS IN CONTROL

CONTEXT

There is no specific Bible verse where these exact words are stated, but this is a frequently spoken phrase that describes God as the final authority in the universe. It is used to give believers the assurance that Satan's attacks and life's challenges have a limit that is controlled by God (see Job 1 and 1 Corinthians 10:13), and it speaks of God ultimately fulfilling His purposes on earth.

POSITIVE

1 Corinthians 10:13 states that we will not be tempted beyond what we can bear – this is a great promise of God's control in our lives. Romans 8:28 also tells us that even the negative things in life can be turned to a positive (through God's control) for those who love God and have responded to His call for us. These are two examples of His positive control in our midst.

CHECKING THE FOUNDATION

There will be a crack in our spiritual foundation if we think "God is in control" means that everything that happens is God's will. God gave control of the earth to man, but Adam gave this authority to Satan in the Garden of Eden. Jesus then came and took the keys of authority from the devil and said to us, "All authority has been given to me; therefore, go..." (Matthew 28:18-19). Matthew 16:15-19 further reveals that the keys of "binding and loosing" have been given to those who walk in the revelation that Jesus is the Christ (the anointed one). As sons and daughters of God, we have been commissioned to control the devil, control the speed of kingdom advancement, and control the level of blessing and protection for our descendants and ourselves.

CONCLUDING THOUGHTS

There are great assurances of God's overall control in our lives, but His control can be limited by us. When we hear, "How could God allow this to happen?" we would be wise to consider the better question: "How could we (the Church) allow this to happen?" We must be careful to not allow the phrase "God is in control" to make us passive and fatalistic.

DISCUSSION QUESTIONS

1. What truth stood out to you the most in this teaching?
2. How have you seen the misunderstanding of God's "control" cause problems in people's beliefs, and what are some solutions?
3. How much control do you believe God has given to men and women on the earth? Explain.

SPEAK THESE DECLARATIONS ALOUD

- God's hand is on my life to protect me and to turn every negative situation to good for me.
- God has delegated His authority to me to bring heaven to earth.
- I have the keys of the kingdom, and I use them to powerfully advance the kingdom.

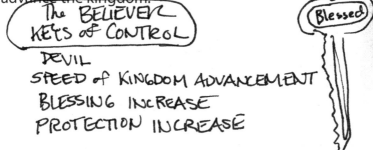

The BELIEVER
KEYS of CONTROL

Blessed

DEVIL
SPEED of KINGDOM ADVANCEMENT
BLESSING INCREASE
PROTECTION INCREASE

6 THE ANSWER TO YOUR PRAYER WILL BE YES, NO, OR WAIT

CONTEXT

This is not a specific Scripture passage, but is a common saying in Christianity.

POSITIVE

James 4:3 says this: "You ask and do not receive, because you ask amiss, that you may spend it on your pleasures." Here is an example where the answer to prayer is no. There are other situations where the answer is delayed because there is a special timing for its manifestation.

CHECKING THE FOUNDATION

We will have a crack in our spiritual foundation if we do not have confidence that our prayers will be answered. 1 John 5:14-15 says we are to have assurance of answered prayer because of a knowing of the will of God. Effective prayer is based largely on God's promises. "For all the promises of God in Him (Jesus) are Yes, and in Him Amen, to the glory of God through us" (2 Corinthians 1:20). Faith believes we receive the answer at the time of prayer. "Therefore I say to you, whatever things you ask when you pray, believe that you receive them, and you will have them" (Mark 11:24). Our belief that we have the answer to our prayer before seeing it is the key to seeing it. If we think that each of our prayers could have a "no" or "wait" answer, then we will be unable to "believe before we see," and we will constantly be passive in prayer (because we will conclude that unchanging circumstances are God's "no" or God's "wait").

CONCLUDING THOUGHTS

The immature Christian will have more "no" answers to prayer because of a lack of knowledge of God's will. The key thing to remember is this: we cannot conclude that the lack of seeing the answer to prayer means that God has said "no" or "wait." To do so would create a huge crack in our faith foundation and rob us from the experience of knowing that we have things before they have manifested.

DISCUSSION QUESTIONS

1. What truth stood out to you the most in this teaching?
2. Do you agree with this statement: "The immature Christian will have more 'no' answers to prayer because of a lack of knowledge of God's will?" Why or why not?
3. What steps can we take to believe that we receive the answer to prayer at the time we pray?

SPEAK THESE DECLARATIONS ALOUD

- I have a powerful prayer life.
- My prayers are powerful and effective.
- ⊙ The moment I receive the answer to prayer is the moment I pray.

My Will
selfish
desires

Gods Will
Knowledge
of Kingdom Promises
1. Pray — recieve it by faith
2. Manefifestation

7 GOD IS SOVEREIGN

CONTEXT

"Oh sovereign Lord" (e.g. Jeremiah 32:17) and other references to God's sovereignty are mentioned many times in the Bible (especially the Old Testament). Sovereign means to have supreme authority or power. God truly is sovereign and is above all others.

POSITIVE

The Christian exults in God's awesome power! In Christ, we have assurance that nothing can snatch us away from God's love or from eternal life with Him. The devil cannot touch that. Satan's power is minuscule compared to the supremacy of our God.

CHECKING THE FOUNDATION

There will be a crack in our spiritual foundation if we believe that "God is sovereign" means that He makes everything happen or that everything that happens is His will. Consider our salvation – "(God) desires all men to be saved" (1 Timothy 2:4). His will is that everyone is saved. Is this "will" happening in every life? No. God's will must be believed, received, and contended for. Just as God's will of salvation does not automatically happen, other "wills" are not guaranteed either (e.g. blessings, protection, provision, long life, etc.). These additional parts of our "promised land" are sovereignly available to all but require a response from us for them to increasingly manifest in our midst. Those who passively sit back and say, "If God wants me to have that, He will give it to me," are going to live far short of God's sovereign best for their lives.

CONCLUDING THOUGHTS

Many are bitter at God because of a misunderstanding of His sovereignty. The "accuser of the brethren" (Satan) first brought accusation against God (we see one example of this in Genesis 3), and he has not stopped today. If he can place a seed of doubt in our minds about God's goodness, then there is a danger of major foundational damage in our lives that will lead to wrong assumptions and wrong choices.

DISCUSSION QUESTIONS

1. What truth stood out to you the most in this teaching?
2. How can we build a positive stronghold of faith in God's goodness?
3. If someone were to say, "God did not stop this disaster; therefore, He is not good," how would you respond?

SPEAK THESE DECLARATIONS ALOUD

- I am receiving increased revelation about God's sovereignty.
- I powerfully release the truth that God is good.
- I am free from bitterness toward God and free others from it as well.

8 WE MUST BE BALANCED IN OUR CHRISTIAN WALK

CONTEXT

This is not a Scripture verse, but we can infer that we are to be balanced in our Christian lives because of seemingly contradictory commands given to us (e.g. be joyful and be serious, have justice and mercy, be prepared and spontaneous, pray and be productive, be administrative and Spirit led, help the needy but don't enable the slothful, etc.).

POSITIVE

Every situation requires specific wisdom from God to understand which truth to apply. Paul adapted his behavior to influence people. "I have made myself a servant to all, that I might win the more; and to the Jews I became as a Jew, that I might win Jews; to those who are under the law, as under the law, that I might win those who are under the law" (1 Corinthians 9:19-21). Paul was a balanced person who said he could respond successfully in the best and worst of circumstances (Philippians 4:11-13). We too can respond in whatever manner is needed to help people and to advance the kingdom.

CHECKING THE FOUNDATION

There will be a crack in our spiritual foundation if we believe the balanced Christian life is a mixture of faith and unbelief, passion and cynicism, or victory and defeat. Many believers want to embrace a little of every doctrinal teaching in order to have an acceptable, balanced Christianity. Unfortunately this will lead to a dilution of power as we try to combine faith in God's promises with traditional explanations for why there is suffering and unanswered prayer. James speaks of this when he says, "A double-minded man is unstable in all his ways" (James 1:8). He is referring to the one who does not believe God will do what He said He would do. To be "crack-free," we must be "unbalanced" toward the belief that God's promises are true.

CONCLUDING THOUGHTS

The value for balance in the Christian lifestyle must not be greater than our "yes" to following God. Many who have feared being considered fanatical concerning the promises of God have fallen to the other extreme of becoming weak, hopeless, and confused. We must avoid both extremes and learn to have healthy balance in our lives.

DISCUSSION QUESTIONS

1. What truth stood out to you the most in this teaching?
2. How is being balanced in life both a positive and negative thing?
3. What truths of God are you choosing to be single minded about (e.g. He is good, He provides, He heals, etc.)?

SPEAK THESE DECLARATIONS ALOUD

- I know what to do in every situation I face.
- Double mindedness has been eradicated from my life.
- I am unshakable in my beliefs that all of God's promises are true.

9   THE PRINCE OF THE KINGDOM OF PERSIA WITHSTOOD ME

CONTEXT

"Then he said to me, 'Do not fear, Daniel, for from the first day that you set your heart to understand, and to humble yourself before your God, your words were heard; and I have come because of your words. But the prince of the kingdom of Persia withstood me twenty-one days; and behold, Michael, one of the chief princes, came to help me, for I had been left alone there with the kings of Persia. Now I have come to make you understand what will happen to your people in the latter days, for the vision refers to many days yet to come'" (Daniel 10:12-14).

POSITIVE

This passage helps us understand there is sometimes spiritual warfare involved in prayer. The prince of Persia was a high-ranking demon who was hindering the answer to prayer. Michael was a high-ranking angel who intervened on Daniel's behalf. It is important, as we pray, to recognize that there is a spirit realm, and our words are affecting more than we can see with our eyes.

CHECKING THE FOUNDATION

There will be a crack in our spiritual foundation if we expect demons to withstand us now in the same manner as in the Old Testament. This event in Daniel happened before the cross and resurrection – at which time Jesus "disarmed principalities and powers... triumphing over them" (Colossians 2:15). The belief that the devil is the same now as in the Old Testament will actually help create a more difficult spiritual experience for us. New Covenant spiritual warfare is not fighting through the devil's resistance, but it is battling through the lies in our mind and heart that stand against the knowledge of the victory that we have in Jesus.

CONCLUDING THOUGHTS

It is true that the devil can be empowered by agreement with him, but he cannot stand or stay when people who know their authority resist him and command him to leave in the name of Jesus. Even though it may take time to see the enemy's influence evicted, it would be wise to believe James 4:7, "Submit to God, resist the devil and he will flee from you," rather than focusing on an Old Testament experience of Daniel.

DISCUSSION QUESTIONS

1. What truth stood out to you the most in this teaching?
2. How much should the devil be emphasized in teachings on spiritual warfare?
3. How would you describe the difference between Old Testament and New Testament spiritual warfare?

SPEAK THESE DECLARATIONS ALOUD

- I have tremendous revelation about spiritual warfare.
- Wherever I go, Satan's influence declines and God's influence increases.
- I am an undevourable Christian.

CONTEXT

Christians often say this to encourage others to look to God and not to people as their source of healing. The Apostle Paul tore his clothes when people started to say he was a god because of all the miracles that were done through him (Acts 14:14). He knew the importance of being a sign that pointed people to Jesus Christ and not to himself.

POSITIVE

It is vital that we learn to give God glory and thanks through Jesus Christ for the great things that are done through us (including healing). Self-exaltation and pride have been the downfall of many (consider Nebuchadnezzar in Daniel 4 and Herod in Acts 12). Jesus said, "Apart from Me, you can do nothing" (John 15:5). Truly, we need to understand that our connection to God the Father through Jesus Christ is the key for divine healing (and all other kingdom benefits) to flow through us.

CHECKING THE FOUNDATION

There will be a crack in our spiritual foundation if we overemphasize God's role in the healing of others and underemphasize our part in the process. Jesus told His disciples to "heal the sick" (Matthew 10:8). The Apostle John told the lame man, "Look at us" (Acts 3:4). God has delegated His authority to us to heal the sick. The biblical model demonstrated in the gospels and Acts for walking in this authority is to declare healing over lives (not ask for healing). The continual asking of God to heal reveals a detrimental crack in our theology that will ultimately limit what is done through us. Too often the phrase "it is God who heals, not me" is used as a form of false humility that lessens personal responsibility and decreases expectation for healing.

CONCLUDING THOUGHTS

Each one of us will have to work out our own philosophy as we walk down the road of bringing healing to others. In doing so, we must focus to stay out of the "ditches" on both sides of this road: false humility and self-exaltation. Truly, we will become part of a new breed of radical believers that have confidence in "the greater works" we will do (John 14:12), and who are passionate to worship Jesus and give Him all the glory.

DISCUSSION QUESTIONS

1. What truth stood out to you the most in this teaching?
2. Why is it important to speak to sickness rather than asking God to heal the sickness?
3. What is the difference between confidence and arrogance in prayer and releasing healing to others?

SPEAK THESE DECLARATIONS ALOUD

- I heal the sick in the name of Jesus.
- I have growing revelation about the power of speaking to things.
- When miracles are done through me, Jesus receives exuberant praise.

11 EVERY TIME I MOVE FORWARD IN GOD, SATAN ATTACKS ME

CONTEXT

These words are frequently heard in churches and in prayer meetings. It is the apparent experience of many.

POSITIVE

The devil hates Christians who seek to advance the kingdom of God. He is prowling around "like a roaring lion seeking whom he may devour" (1 Peter 5:8). It would be foolish for us to ignore the fact that we "wrestle not against flesh and blood, but against principalities, against powers, against the rulers of the darkness of this age..." (Ephesians 6:12). It would likewise be foolish for us to forget that "He who is in you is greater than he who is in the world" (1 John 4:4).

CHECKING THE FOUNDATION

There will be a crack in our spiritual foundation if we put more faith in Satan's power to attack us than in God's power to protect us. If we believe that the attacks of Satan (with their negative results) are normal, then our expectation of this will actually attract those things to our lives (and will reinforce this lie as truth to us). Jesus said, "According to your faith, so be it" (Matthew 9:29). Those who believe they are protected will increasingly experience protection in their lives. Those who believe they will be attacked after moving forward in God (or in ministry) will increasingly have this experience in their lives.

CONCLUDING THOUGHTS

Sometimes we overemphasize things like, "If the devil is not causing you problems, then you are not a threat to him." There is some truth in this statement, but it too often creates a crack of believing that difficulty is the true sign of spirituality. Yes, the devil is looking for those he may devour, but he can only devour when there is agreement with him or fear of him. As people of hope and victory, we are to speak more about God's wonderful protection than we do about Satan's attacks and lies. As we do so, we will increasingly see that protection manifest in our lives.

DISCUSSION QUESTIONS

1. What truth stood out to you the most in this teaching?
2. Do you agree or disagree with the assumption that those who are moving forward in God will experience more spiritual attacks in their lives than those who are not moving forward? Why or why not?
3. How have you experienced the Lord's protection as you have moved forward in Him?

SPEAK THESE DECLARATIONS ALOUD

- I walk under a supernatural protection.
- Higher level angels join me as I go to higher levels in God.
- I have great beliefs about spiritual warfare.

12 GIVE TO HIM WHO ASKS YOU

CONTEXT

"You have heard that it was said, 'An eye for an eye and a tooth for a tooth.' But I tell you not to resist an evil person. But whoever slaps you on your right cheek, turn the other to him also. If anyone wants to sue you and take away your tunic, let him have your cloak also. And whoever compels you to go one mile, go with him two. Give to him who asks you, and from him who wants to borrow from you do not turn away" (Matthew 5:38-42).

POSITIVE

In the Beatitudes (Matthew 5-7), Jesus upgrades the type of attitudes the people of God should have. He focuses on heart issues rather than the Old Covenant's emphasis on outward obedience. In the passage above, Jesus is confronting the spirit of revenge and the tendency to overly protect ourselves from being done wrong in life. Both of these attitudes reflect a lack of trust in God providing for us in the future.

CHECKING THE FOUNDATION

There will be a crack in our spiritual foundation and our ability to influence many if we consistently let the urgent demands and needs of others dictate our daily priorities. The commands in Matthew 5 must be understood in cooperation with other biblical truths and priorities (e.g. family responsibilities, the Sabbath principle, other commitments that we have already made, contracts we have signed, etc.). Those who try to meet every need around them will end up in lack in finances, relationships, health, spirituality, and potentially in many other areas.

CONCLUDING THOUGHTS

We all must be willing to give what we have to others, but we cannot let the emotions of the moment regularly blind us to what God has told us in the past or from the commitments we have made. For example, paying off our debts or being faithful in tithing to our local church may not seem as important as giving to a homeless person, but it is a key part of getting our priorities in order (which will eventually enable us to help more people in the long run).

DISCUSSION QUESTIONS

1. What truth stood out to you the most in this teaching?
2. How can you steward your wealth now for a lifetime of generosity?
3. Would you say that some people (Including yourself) give too much or too little? Please explain.

SPEAK THESE DECLARATIONS ALOUD

- I am a very generous person.
- I live a life of incredible wisdom and know how much to give in every situation.
- I know when to give and when not to give to someone who asks.

13 DO GOOD, HOPING FOR NOTHING IN RETURN

CONTEXT

"And if you lend to those from whom you hope to receive back, what credit is that to you?... But love your enemies, do good, and lend, hoping for nothing in return; and your reward will be great..." (Luke 6:34-35).

POSITIVE

In this passage, Jesus is calling us to a higher way of living. He is rebuking the "I'll do something for you if you do something for me" syndrome. We must look to God to meet our needs, and thus resist the temptation to expect things back from those we have given something to.

CHECKING THE FOUNDATION

There will be a crack in our spiritual foundation if we do not believe that our giving will cause an increase in what we receive in this life. Later in Luke 6:38 it says, "Give, and it will be given to you: good measure, pressed down, shaken together, and running over will be put into your bosom. For with the same measure that you use, it will be measured back to you." Besides this verse, there are many other Bible passages that exhort us to give with expectancy that we will receive a blessing from our generosity. "He who sows sparingly will also reap sparingly, and he who sows bountifully will also reap bountifully" (2 Corinthians 9:6), "Whatever a man sows, that he will also reap" (Galatians 6:7), and "Judge not, and you shall not be judged. Condemn not, and you shall not be condemned. Forgive, and you will be forgiven. Give, and it will be given to you..." (Luke 6:37-38). Scripture makes it clear that we are to anticipate increase from God in this life when we give.

CONCLUDING THOUGHTS

It is wrong to give to others with the motive to get something back from them. It is, however, just as wrong to not expect to receive back from God when we have given. Indeed, God's law of sowing and reaping is one of the basic spiritual laws that we are to use to create an abundance in many ways to give to others.

DISCUSSION QUESTIONS

1. What truth stood out to you the most in this teaching?
2. Is it wrong to give with expectation to receive something from God in return? Please explain.
3. What can you do to increase your expectancy of receiving a great harvest for your giving?

SPEAK THESE DECLARATIONS ALOUD

- I sow abundant seeds into the spirit realm and reap a great harvest as a result.
- I do not expect something back from those to whom I have given.
- I have great understanding of the spiritual law of sowing and reaping.

14 DO ALL SPEAK WITH TONGUES?

CONTEXT

"And God has appointed these in the church: first apostles, second prophets, third teachers, after that miracles, then gifts of healings, helps, administrations, varieties of tongues. Are all apostles? Are all prophets? Are all teachers? Are all workers of miracles? Do all have gifts of healing? Do all speak with tongues? Do all interpret? But earnestly desire the best gifts" (1 Corinthians 12:28-31a). These verses emphasize diversity in the body of Christ.

POSITIVE

In this chapter, Paul reveals different roles Christians have in the body of Christ. Individual believers are to find their unique place in His church and honor others for theirs. With this in mind, there will be those who are more prone to operate in miracles, healing, public messages in tongues, and in interpreting messages in tongues.

CHECKING THE FOUNDATION

There will be a crack in our spiritual foundation if we believe that some of the gifts are not for us. This false belief will cause passiveness in seeking breakthrough of the miraculous in us and through us. We will thus fall prey to using our own experiences to create our identity and our doctrinal beliefs, rather than God's promises. In the passage we are considering here (1 Corinthians 12:30), Paul is referring to "public tongues" that would occur in a corporate meeting. He cannot mean that speaking in tongues is only for a select few because: 1) We are commanded to earnestly desire spiritual gifts (tongues is one of these – 1 Corinthians 14:1). 2) Tongues is a key to building our faith (1 Corinthians 14:4, Jude 20). 3) Tongues is part of the armor of God (1 Corinthians 14:14,15 and Ephesians 6:18).

CONCLUDING THOUGHTS

Oh, what a big weakness this little crack can cause! If we believe God sovereignly gives some people certain gifts (and does not do so for others), then we will live in perpetual limitation concerning our potential and destiny. Our experience cannot create our beliefs about God or ourselves.

DISCUSSION QUESTIONS

1. What truth stood out to you the most in this teaching?
2. Why do you think some Christians conclude that God has only given them the spiritual gifts that are operating in their lives?
3. Why is it a problem to use past experience to determine our identity and spiritual gifts?

SPEAK THESE DECLARATIONS ALOUD

- Like the Apostle Paul, I am zealous in speaking in tongues.
- I have growing revelation about the power in tongues.
- I have full access to every spiritual gift.

15 A THORN IN THE FLESH WAS GIVEN TO ME

CONTEXT

"And lest I should be exalted above measure by the abundance of the revelations, a thorn in the flesh was given to me, a messenger of Satan to buffet me, lest I be exalted above measure. Concerning this thing I pleaded with the Lord three times that it might depart from me. And He said to me, 'My grace is sufficient for you, for My strength is made perfect in weakness'" (2 Corinthians 12:7-9).

POSITIVE

Paul had tremendous revelation, powerful spiritual experiences, and great boldness. He was a big threat to the enemy; therefore, the devil sent a "messenger" (most likely in the form of persecution from people) to harass him. Even so, God's grace was sufficient for Paul to be an overcomer (even if this "problem" did not immediately leave).

CHECKING THE FOUNDATION

There will be a crack in our spiritual foundation if we believe that this thorn was a "messenger from God" instead of a "messenger from Satan" (as is clearly stated). If we assume the thorn is a "messenger from God," it will cause us to not put up a fight against Satan's assignments against us. Even though we don't know the exact nature of Paul's thorn, we do know it was from the devil and Scripture teaches us that we must take authority over the devil with persistent and confident resistance (James 4:7).

CONCLUDING THOUGHTS

Why did Paul ask God to remove this demonic thorn instead of dealing with it directly? We do not know the full story here, but we need to be careful in our conclusions. This thorn passage and the story of Job are exceptions to the overall scriptural themes of the power of faith and the power of man's authority over the weapons of Satan. In our study of these passages, we must consider the overall teaching of the Bible on these subjects, and not rely on religious tradition in our interpretations.

DISCUSSION QUESTIONS

1. What truth stood out to you the most in this teaching?
2. Have traditional interpretations about Paul's thorn in the flesh created problems in the body of Christ? Please explain.
3. What do you think of the author's explanation about Paul's thorn in the flesh and why?

SPEAK THESE DECLARATIONS ALOUD

- When I resist the devil, he flees from me.
- It is clear to me what I need to resist in Jesus' name.
- I have great compassion for those who are battling a similar experience to Paul's.

16 I AM CLAIMING MY HEALING BY FAITH

CONTEXT

This phrase is not a specific Scripture passage, but it is stated by many Christians when pain and symptoms of sickness are still present in their lives, and they are believing for healing.

POSITIVE

Many Bible verses support the concept of "claiming" that we are who God says we are, and we have what He says we have, even before it has manifested in our lives and circumstances. Joel 3:10, for example, states, "Let the weak say I am strong." We are to claim strength even in the face of manifested weakness. Romans 4:17 gives us further insight: "God, who gives life to the dead and calls those things which do not exist as though they did." Concerning healing, Peter urges us to have a personal identity of health and as a healed one when he says, "by whose stripes you were healed" (1 Peter 2:24).

CHECKING THE FOUNDATION

There will be a crack in our spiritual foundation if we use the formula of claiming healing without attempting to increase our measure of faith through a deeper revelation of God's love, character, and promises. Our faith declaration is an important component of our health, but it needs to be mixed with a strong pursuit of God as well. Also, if we are in a healing meeting, and we verbalize a claim of healing before it has fully manifested in us, we may block further needed ministry from those God has brought to us. Even Jesus prayed for someone more than once (Mark 8:22-25).

CONCLUDING THOUGHTS

"Naming it and claiming it" was a common phrase in Christianity in the 1980's. It was a truth that catapulted many people to receive the benefits of the cross, but this truth was also abused (because of an overemphasis on spoken faith and an underemphasis on other important spiritual laws). Wise Christians consistently call themselves healed, but they don't limit their divine health plan to just their confession. They continue to seek God and His promises, and listen to what He is saying specifically to them.

DISCUSSION QUESTIONS

1. What truth stood out to you the most in this teaching?
2. When is claiming our healing by faith a good thing? When is it not?
3. What are ways to encourage others to continue contending for their healing until it fully manifests?

SPEAK THESE DECLARATIONS ALOUD

- The pursuit of God is my highest priority.
- I make room for spiritual laws to be activated in my life.
- I have a powerful strategy to walk in physical health.

CONTEND for MANIFESTATION

PURSUE GOD'S VOICE IN MY JOURNEY OF VISION LOSS etc.

"STAY OPEN" TO ASK FOR PRAYER WHEN THE HOLY SPIRIT PROMPTS

RECIEVE PRAYER from OTHERS WHEN THEY ARE PROMPTED TO PRAY FOR ME.

33

17 ALL RELIGIONS HAVE TRUTH IN THEM

CONTEXT

This is not a Bible verse, but it is a statement commonly heard.

POSITIVE

God has established spiritual laws that are true, no matter who declares or practices them. Most religions understand the blessing that comes from obeying laws of the spirit such as honesty, sexual fidelity, self control, kindness, generosity, tithing, hard work, meditation, keeping covenant, protecting our children, honoring marriage, having wholesome friends, meeting regularly with like-minded believers, etc. They also generally understand that there is a curse released when these spiritual laws are violated. Therefore, most or all religions have truth in them because they rightly recognize that moral choices dramatically influence the quality of life for our descendants and ourselves.

CHECKING THE FOUNDATION

There will be a crack in our spiritual foundation if we believe that all roads lead to heaven and that all religions are a path to God. Common sense should tell us this. (Do all roads lead to San Francisco?) There will be a level of blessing on many religions (because of an honoring of spiritual laws), but we must be careful to not let that blessing deceive us into assuming that they lead to the truth. Indeed, truth is a person, not a life philosophy. Jesus said, "I am the way, the truth, and the life; no one comes to Father except through Me" (John 14:6). Religion urges man to attempt to reach a higher spiritual place by prioritizing the spirit realm, while Christianity invites man into relationship with the person who is truth. The difference is night and day.

CONCLUDING THOUGHTS

Because of a narrow interpretation of the Bible, Christians sometimes reject powerful spiritual laws that other religions have discovered. The church can learn from other religions to understand God more fully. This openness though cannot undermine the reality that only Jesus (through His sinless life) was able to enter into the spirit realm to: 1) disarm and defeat demonic forces and give the keys of spiritual authority back to men and women, 2) satisfy God's justice concerning our personal sin, and 3) open a way to a relationship with God for now and for eternity.

DISCUSSION QUESTIONS

1. What truth stood out to you the most in this teaching?
2. Do you agree with the idea that a narrow interpretation of the Bible has caused some Christians to reject powerful spiritual laws that other religions have discovered? Why or why not?
3. What makes Jesus different than every other religious leader who has ever lived?

SPEAK THESE DECLARATIONS ALOUD

- Jesus is the way, the truth, and the life. No one comes to the Father except through Him.
- My understanding of God's spiritual laws is increasing, and as a result, my life is blessed more and more.
- I am an influential evangelist for Christ.

18 WILL YOU PRAY FOR MY HEALING?

CONTEXT

This is a common prayer request. James 5:14-15 supports this when it says, "Is anyone among you sick? Let him call for the elders of the church, and let them pray over him, anointing him with oil in the name of the Lord. And the prayer of faith will save (heal) the sick."

POSITIVE

It is a wonderful thing to be able to pray for people and to have people pray for us. James says that the sick are to call for the elders of the church to "pray the prayer of faith" over them. Those who understand that healing is a "benefit" (Psalms 103:3) and vital part of our salvation (Isaiah 53:3-4) will indeed "pray the prayer of faith" concerning sickness.

CHECKING THE FOUNDATION

There will be a crack in our spiritual foundation if we think that we are to ask God to heal people. Jesus never asked the Father to heal others, and the apostles didn't either. They prayed in faith by "speaking to" bodies and declaring healing over lives. They realized that healing was already part of their covenant with God, and they were to release it by faith (and not ask for what had already been given to them). We will have a crack in our foundation if we are unsure if God wants to heal.

CONCLUDING THOUGHTS

It is good to pray for people to be blessed, to walk in health, and to have personal breakthrough. We must also grow in "praying the prayer of faith." We will impact lives (and see increased health and miracles) as we believe in our authority as Christians. "Therefore He who supplies the Spirit to you and works miracles among you, does He do it by the works of the law, or by the hearing of faith?" (Galatians 3:5). Let's keep hearing the good news: Jesus purchased healing, and we have the glorious privilege of giving this free gift to everyone we can.

DISCUSSION QUESTIONS

1. What truth stood out to you the most in this teaching?
2. What beliefs are needed for us to proclaim healing rather than asking God to heal someone?
3. In what areas are we to make declarations (to enforce the victory of Christ) instead of asking for things?

SPEAK THESE DECLARATIONS ALOUD

- I pray the prayer of faith and see people healed regularly.
- Declaring healing is part of my prayer of faith.
- I have wisdom to know when to ask God for things in prayer and when to make a declaration.

19 WHAT ABOUT JOB?

CONTEXT

"Then the LORD said to Satan, 'Have you considered My servant Job, that there is none like him on the earth...' So Satan answered the LORD and said, 'Does Job fear God for nothing? Have You not made a hedge around him, around his household, and around all that he has on every side?... But now, stretch out Your hand and touch all that he has, and he will surely curse You to Your face!' And the LORD said to Satan, 'Behold, all that he has is in your power; only do not lay a hand on his person.' So Satan went out from the presence of the LORD" (see Job 1:8-12).

POSITIVE

Job loved God in the midst of great problems and tragedy. He is an example to us of being steadfast in extremely difficult circumstances.

CHECKING THE FOUNDATION

There will be a crack in our spiritual foundation if we conclude that God allows Satan to test our Christian love and commitment through destructive loss of property, death of family members, and physical affliction. If we believe this (even to a small degree), we will live in doubt concerning God's goodness and His will about protection, long life, and physical health. The devil (the thief) is seeking "to kill, steal, and destroy" things in our lives (see John 10:10). We are called to resist the devil to the point where he flees from us (James 4:7). If we think that God has indirectly sent him to us to test our lives, we will have little power or faith to persevere in our resistance of him (because we will think we might be resisting God).

CONCLUDING THOUGHTS

Job said, "What I greatly feared has come upon me" (Job 3:25). His fear gave Satan legal access to "kill, steal, and destroy." God "allowed" this attack only in the sense that He has established spiritual laws (such as the laws of fear and faith) that bring a result into our lives. Job's situation was not a random or sovereign attack; it manifested because of a violation of a spiritual law. We will be on a "slippery slope" if we subconsciously believe that God might sovereignly dismantle our lives to test us.

DISCUSSION QUESTIONS

1. What truth stood out to you the most in this teaching?
2. What do you think of the author's conclusions about the reasons for the calamity Job faced?
3. What can we do to see increased protection on our families and nations?

SPEAK THESE DECLARATIONS ALOUD

- I remain faithful to God no matter what happens in my life.
- God is a good parent in my life. I can trust Him.
- Jesus came that I might have life and life more abundantly. I am experiencing this abundant life more and more.

20 THE LOVE OF MONEY IS THE ROOT OF ALL KINDS OF EVIL

CONTEXT

"But those who desire to be rich fall into temptation and a snare, and into many foolish and harmful lusts which drown men in destruction and perdition. For the love of money is a root of all kinds of evil, for which some have strayed from the faith in their greediness, and pierced themselves through with many sorrows" (1 Timothy 6:9-10).

POSITIVE

Financial considerations are important in decision making, but if we do not submit them to spiritual and family priorities, we are going to have trouble. When making decisions, our primary question needs to be "How will this decision affect my spiritual life and family life?" If money becomes our greatest love, then we will compromise spiritual laws (e.g. honesty, honoring people, family commitments, generosity, seeking God's kingdom first, etc.), and we will reap a negative harvest as a result. It is not money itself that is the root of evil; it is the love of money. When Jesus said, "You cannot serve God and mammon" (Matthew 6:24), He empowered us to choose where we aim our true affections.

CHECKING THE FOUNDATION

There will be a crack in our spiritual foundation if we do not expect and contend for increased financial wealth as we move forward in God. Jesus commanded us in Matthew 28:18-20 to go and transform the world in His name. There is no way we can do this without prosperity. It takes a lot of money to evangelize and disciple the world. We cannot just take care of our own needs, but we must tenaciously go after God's laws of financial increase to impact the world. This indeed will help us be obedient to the Great Commission of Matthew 28.

CONCLUDING THOUGHTS

We are to resist the temptation of fearing increased wealth in our lives. It is true that many are ruined by the love of money, and it is true that we must constantly guard our soul from its destructive influence; but we cannot go to the other extreme of believing that poverty is true spirituality. As we grow in Christ, we should expect "an abundance for every good work" to be our testimony (2 Corinthians 9:8-12). There will be multitudes in heaven that will be glad we did.

DISCUSSION QUESTIONS

1. What truth stood out to you the most in this teaching?
2. Do you believe God has sovereignly chosen how financially blessed you are, or do you believe it is up to you to determine that? Please explain.
3. What beliefs and actions are needed to live in abundance?

SPEAK THESE DECLARATIONS ALOUD

- I have an abundance for every good work.
- I am very blessed in my finances.
- I have healthy attitudes about money.

BELIEVE ABUNDANCE FOLLOWS MY OBEDIENCE TO FULFILL GOD'S PURPOSES THROUGH MY LIFE.

BEHAVE WITH "AN ABUNDANCE MINDSET"

21 WE WILL NEVER UNDERSTAND ALL THE MYSTERIES OF GOD

CONTEXT

This phrase is not in the Bible, but can be inferred from many Bible passages. One example is from Isaiah 55:8-9: "'For My thoughts are not your thoughts, nor are your ways My ways,' says the LORD. 'For as the heavens are higher than the earth, so are My ways higher than your ways, and My thoughts than your thoughts.'"

POSITIVE

It is vital that we as Christians learn to live with mystery and not think we have to have an explanation for everything in life. When difficult and mysterious things happen, we should be comfortable in saying, "I don't know why this happened, but one thing that I do know is this: any God who would send His only Son to die for us is good – very good." Also, it is vital to know that the unresolved, mysterious happenings of life often have a "door" of revelation attached to them concerning new understanding of God and His goodness. This door can be passed through as we overcome bitterness and the temptation to create our doctrine (concept of God) from our negative experiences.

CHECKING THE FOUNDATION

There will be a crack in our spiritual foundation if we allow the "God is mysterious" thinking to lead us to a place where we subconsciously conclude that everything that happens is His will. "After all," we might say, "God may have a reason for why he wants this person left sick, or in lack, or to have that accident, or to experience that abuse, or to die early in life." That conclusion will hinder our ability to pray in confident faith because we might be coming against a mysterious thing that God is doing.

CONCLUDING THOUGHTS

We realize that there are often other factors to be addressed besides prayer and faith to see God's will manifest, but we need to be cautious to not use "God is mysterious" theology as an excuse for why we are not resisting Satan's "stealing, killing, and destroying." Do our beliefs lead us to fatalism, hopelessness, and passivity, or do they lead us to a burning and sacrificial realization that we can change history and the world in the name of Jesus? How we interpret the mysteriousness of God will be a huge factor in what direction we take.

DISCUSSION QUESTIONS

1. What truth stood out to you the most in this teaching?
2. How do we maintain strong beliefs while still embracing mystery in our Christian walk?
3. What kind of beliefs are at the root of why some Christians currently walk in fatalism, hopelessness, and passivity?

SPEAK THESE DECLARATIONS ALOUD

- Because I trust in God's goodness, I don't need to have an answer for why everything happens.
- I weaken the enemy's ability to steal, kill, and destroy because I have strong beliefs.
- I do not lean on my own understanding in my relationship with God, but I trust in Him with all my heart.

22 SPIRITUAL WARFARE IS MAINLY DEALING WITH THE DEVIL

CONTEXT

This phrase is not in Scripture, but a logical conclusion from passages including: "Behold, I give you the authority to trample on serpents and scorpions, and over all the power of the enemy, and nothing shall by any means hurt you" (Luke 10:19), "Resist the devil and he will flee from you" (James 4:7), and "For we do not wrestle against flesh and blood, but against principalities, against powers, against the rulers of the darkness of this age, against spiritual hosts of wickedness in the heavenly places" (Ephesians 6:12).

POSITIVE

It is foolish to ignore the devil's existence. The Bible is clear that there are forces of darkness that are seeking to oppose the advancement of God's kingdom. We can become aware of the tactics of the enemy and learn how to walk in victory over him. We can be courageous in this process – "For God has not given us a spirit of fear, but of power and of love and of a sound mind" (2 Timothy 1:7).

CHECKING THE FOUNDATION

We will have a crack in our spiritual foundation if we think that spiritual warfare is primarily beating up the devil; Jesus already did this on the cross. Our main warfare is battling our own thoughts rather than fighting Satan. This truth is supported by the main spiritual warfare passage in the Bible, 2 Corinthians 10:4-5 – "For the weapons of our warfare are not carnal but mighty in God for pulling down strongholds, casting down arguments and every high thing that exalts itself against the knowledge of God, bringing every thought into captivity to the obedience of Christ." The only instruction that is given for how to pull down strongholds is the "capturing" of every lying thought.

CONCLUDING THOUGHTS

The anointing of God flowing through His people can break the yoke of Satan's hold on lives. This freedom, however, will only be temporary if our beliefs remain in agreement with Satan's lies (even after a powerful encounter with the Holy Spirit). The real battle is in our minds. As we renew our minds with God's victory over Satan and replace lies with truth, we will walk in increasing victory and bring freedom to others.

DISCUSSION QUESTIONS

1. What truth stood out to you the most in this teaching?
2. Jesus already beat the devil on the cross. How does this phrase personally affect you and your view of spiritual warfare?
3. What thoughts might you need to begin taking captive today? What are practical steps for doing this?

SPEAK THESE DECLARATIONS ALOUD

- I am not dumb about the devil, but I choose to focus on the Lord's victory.
- As I renew my mind daily, the kingdom is advancing in and through me.
- I live in ever-increasing freedom, and I bring freedom to others.

23 THE LORD GIVES, AND THE LORD TAKES AWAY

CONTEXT

Job had just lost most of his family due to disaster, and his health was also in a crisis. In response to this he said: "Naked I came from my mother's womb, and naked shall I return there. The LORD gave, and the LORD has taken away; blessed be the name of the LORD" (Job 1:21-22).

POSITIVE

Job is an example to us of worshiping and trusting God in the toughest of times. Paul and Silas also did this in Acts 16:25.

CHECKING THE FOUNDATION

There will be a crack in our spiritual foundation if we believe that God can, and sometimes will, "take away" our family, our health, our finances, and our possessions as part of His plan for our lives. This crack will exist whether we believe that God directly takes these things, or if we believe he "allows" the devil to take them. Either of these belief systems will result in a double mindedness in prayer and faith. In addition to this, Job's conclusion that "the Lord takes away" was an analysis that is inconsistent with basic spiritual laws as set forth in Scripture. When God said in Job 1:12, "Behold, all that he has is in your power," He was more likely stating a reality that already existed (because of Job's fear – see Job 3:25), than a granting of permission to attack Job. Any other conclusion would lead to hopelessness, prayerlessness, and fatalism.

CONCLUDING THOUGHTS

We know God inspired all of Scripture, but not every quote of the people in the Bible are God's thoughts (e.g. Solomon's words in Ecclesiastes). Job's attitude of loving and blessing God during the hardest of times is powerful and is an example for us. We should not, however, allow Job's experience and conclusions formulate our beliefs concerning the reason for negative things in life. If we accept a theology that "the Lord gives and the Lord takes away" in the areas of our health, protection, and loved ones, then there can be little faith in prayer. This would not be in harmony with the message of the New Testament.

DISCUSSION QUESTIONS

1. What truth stood out to you the most in this teaching?
2. What do you admire about Job?
3. "If our interpretation of Scripture does not lead to hope, then we need to question our interpretation." Do you agree or disagree with this statement and why?

SPEAK THESE DECLARATIONS ALOUD

- My doctrinal beliefs are constantly becoming more in line with truth.
- I am gifted in rightly understanding Scripture.
- I worship and trust God in even the most difficult of times.

24 GOD WILL DO IT IN HIS TIME

CONTEXT

"To everything there is a season, a time for every purpose under heaven: a time to be born, and a time to die; a time to plant, and a time to pluck what is planted; a time to kill, and a time to heal; a time to break down, and a time to build up; a time to weep, and a time to laugh; a time to mourn, and a time to dance" (Ecclesiastes 3:1-8). "Therefore humble yourselves under the mighty hand of God, that He may exalt you in due time, casting all your care upon Him, for He cares for you" (1 Peter 5:6-7).

POSITIVE

God's timing is important for us to understand. The principle of "seedtime and harvest" reveals there is a time to plant a seed in every aspect of our lives, and then we wait in faith (without anxious care) for our "due time" to experience its harvest. Also, concerning God's timing, we realize He moves people and events to a "perfect timing" in response to prayer and faith.

CHECKING THE FOUNDATION

There will be a crack in our spiritual foundation if we believe that God has a blueprint plan that He is implementing which has nothing to do with the actions, prayers and beliefs of people. It is important to acknowledge that our choices and beliefs can speed up, slow down, or stop God's will. Consider what happened in Jesus' home town in Mark 6. 2 Peter 3:11-12 speaks of this concerning the last days, "Since all these things will be dissolved, what manner of persons ought you to be in holy conduct and godliness, looking for and hastening the coming of the day of God." We can influence the timing of Christ's return, just as Jesus' mother hastened the time of when her Son was going to start doing miracles (John 2).

CONCLUDING THOUGHTS

Doing the right thing at the wrong time is a problem, just as it is foolish to ignore God's timing in our lives and circumstances. It is also silly to sit back and wait for God to do what He has commissioned us to do. God's timing truly has a lot to do with us. His "will" has more to do with our involvement in an event, than a specific "something" to happen at a certain time.

DISCUSSION QUESTIONS

1. What truth stood out to you the most in this teaching?
2. What are unhealthy beliefs concerning God's timing in our lives? What are healthy beliefs in this area?
3. What can you do to accelerate the timetable of spiritual realities being manifested through your life?

SPEAK THESE DECLARATIONS ALOUD

- I trust God profoundly in His timing for my life.
- Like Jesus' mother, I speed up the timing of miracles and the manifestation of breakthrough.
- I pull events reserved for the future into the present.

25 THE GREATEST AMONG YOU WILL BE YOUR SERVANT

CONTEXT

"But he who is greatest among you shall be your servant. And whoever exalts himself will be humbled, and he who humbles himself will be exalted" (Matthew 20:26-28). "Whoever wishes to be great among you must be your servant, and whoever wishes to be first among you must be your slave; just as the Son of Man came not to be served but to serve" (Matthew 23:11-12).

POSITIVE

Everyone must have a servant's heart. No Christian can ever come to the place where he or she is too spiritual to be a servant. We are to serve in practical, helpful ways, but we also recognize that we are to give our lives fully to Christ to serve people's need of salvation, deliverance, healing, provision, purpose, and family restoration.

CHECKING THE FOUNDATION

There will be a crack in our spiritual foundation if we believe that "servanthood" means that we are only to wait for God's commands before we think, dream, or act. Jesus said in John 15:15, "No longer do I call you servants... but I have called you friends." David was a friend of God, and he wanted to build a temple for his Friend. "'I chose David to be over My people Israel.' Now it was in the heart of my father David to build a temple for the name of the LORD God of Israel. But the LORD said to my father David, 'Whereas it was in your heart to build a temple for My name, you did well that it was in your heart'" (1 Kings 8:16-18). There was a co-laboring between a dedicated person and God.

CONCLUDING THOUGHTS

Psalm 37:4 says, "Delight yourself also in the LORD, And He shall give you the desires of your heart." It is necessary to be a servant, but it is also vital to know that God does not intend for us to be spiritual robots. We are to increasingly trust our ideas and instincts as we live out John 15:7. "If you abide in Me, and My words abide in you, you will ask what you desire, and it shall be done for you."

DISCUSSION QUESTIONS

1. What truth stood out to you the most in this teaching?
2. How do you prioritize serving in your Christian life?
3. Why is it important that we move from a servant relationship to a friend relationship with God? What are the signs we are walking as a friend of God?

SPEAK THESE DECLARATIONS ALOUD

- I am a strong servant in the body of Christ.
- God calls me His friend and partners with my ideas and desires so that the kingdom can advance.
- Because I delight myself in the Lord, He gives me the desires of my heart.

26 CHRISTIANS MUST GO THROUGH A WILDERNESS EXPERIENCE

CONTEXT

Many Bible leaders went through a "wilderness experience" of personal difficulty before they realized their destiny. Moses, David, Abraham, Jacob, Joseph, and others went through a time of the breaking of their self will and a seeming "death of their dreams" for the future. Many today teach that we too must go through similar times in our lives.

POSITIVE

The Children of Israel had to kill giants that were blocking the Promised Land. They were to move through the wilderness to battle and defeat these deceptive beings that were standing between them and their inheritance. Each of us must also take the truth that we have heard on spiritual mountaintops and move through a "valley" (wilderness) of contrary-looking circumstances where we defeat the giants of old thought patterns that have kept us intimidated and defeated. These happenings can teach us to trust God, to release personal agendas, to have pride reduced from our lives, and to move from "formula Christianity" to having a deep and intimate relationship with our God.

CHECKING THE FOUNDATION

There will be a crack in our spiritual foundation if we think that the "wilderness" is a difficult time sent by God to break us, instead of "a swimming upstream" against old thought currents. Those who believe that negative circumstances are what "break us" (and make us usable) will actually attract this kind of experience. God did not call the Children of Israel to spend forty years in the wilderness. Their unbelief and word curses kept them there. Many Christians today are stuck in similar happenings and mistakenly think it is God's will. Remember, Jesus only spent 40 days in the wilderness. He came out by resisting the enemy by speaking inspired truth that He had "hid in His heart" (see Matthew 4).

CONCLUDING THOUGHTS

Every person needs to "find God" personally. We cannot ride on the coat tails of others. We are to pursue learning how to have personal victory in tough and dry circumstances. With that said, we also need to know that the length of our stay in the desert is largely up to us. Will it be forty years? Or will we, like Jesus, speak the Word and find the way to get out of the wilderness?

DISCUSSION QUESTIONS

1. What truth stood out to you the most in this teaching?
2. What beliefs could lessen the length of a wilderness experience? What beliefs would actually increase the time we spend in spiritual deserts?
3. What are ways a believer can increase intimacy with God?

SPEAK THESE DECLARATIONS ALOUD

- God does powerful things in me during every season of my life, including challenging ones.
- I have a deep, intimate relationship with Jesus.
- My beliefs lessen the length of any spiritual wilderness times I may experience.

27 YOU DID NOT HAVE ENOUGH FAITH TO BE HEALED

CONTEXT

"Now He (Jesus) could do no mighty work there (in his home town), except that He laid His hands on a few sick people and healed them. And He marveled because of their unbelief" (Mark 6:5-6).

POSITIVE

1 John 5:4 gives us a key to walking in victory, which includes our health: "For whatever is born of God overcomes the world. And this is the victory that has overcome the world – our faith." It would be foolish to discount the role of faith concerning the advancement of God's kingdom promises in our lives. Jesus frequently spoke of the power of faith in seeing healing and wholeness manifest. One classic passage is in Mark 9 where a father implores Jesus to help his son – "'But if You can do anything, have compassion on us and help us.' Jesus said to him, 'If you can believe, all things are possible to him who believes.'" The man then understood his role in the process and immediately cried out and said with tears, "Lord, I believe; help my unbelief!"

CHECKING THE FOUNDATION

There will be a crack in our spiritual foundation if we overemphasize the role of personal faith and underemphasize additional important factors concerning healing such as: 1) Corporate faith – Jesus called the disciples in Mark 9 a faithless generation when they were unable to help the man's son. He did not rebuke the boy or the father, but he did chastise the disciples for the lack of healing/deliverance. 2) Spiritual laws that need to be addressed beside faith – forgiveness, eliminating self-imposed word curses, etc. 3) The need for perseverance – those believing for healing for themselves and others need to contend for its manifestation without complicating matters by making concluding statements about there being a lack of faith.

CONCLUDING THOUGHTS

Faith is vital and important for healing, but we must make a greater emphasis of celebrating faith's growth rather than focusing on its apparent lack in lives.

DISCUSSION QUESTIONS

1. What truth stood out to you the most in this teaching?
2. How can we inspire people around us to greater faith, and stay away from criticism or condemnation for an apparent lack of faith?
3. Besides believing for healing, what are other things we can do or believe which increase the likelihood of healing manifesting in our lives?

SPEAK THESE DECLARATIONS ALOUD

- I am a person of great faith.
- I have a marvelous understanding of the dynamics that lead to healing in lives.
- Because my faith works through love, I bring healing to body, soul, and spirit.

28 WE ARE LIVING IN THE LAST DAYS

CONTEXT

Matthew 24:42-44 is a passage that points us to a last days attitude. "Watch therefore, for you do not know what hour your Lord is coming. But know this, that if the master of the house had known what hour the thief would come, he would have watched and not allowed his house to be broken into. Therefore you also be ready, for the Son of Man is coming at an hour you do not expect."

POSITIVE

Just as a person close to death is much more likely to concentrate on what is really important in life, there can be a powerful motivation toward urgency and godly focus if we think that we have a limited amount of days left.

CHECKING THE FOUNDATION

There will be a crack in our spiritual foundation if we allow a last days emphasis to create fatalism in us about the future. This crack will grow wider if we unconsciously expect things to get worse around us in the end times (for our lives, our families, our communities, our nation, and for the world). We will find that we are unable to believe God for revival in the nations of the world. Instead of believing and tenaciously claiming Psalms 2:8 for the people of the world ("Ask of Me and I will give you the nations for your inheritance"), we will have uncertainty in our intercession. If the enemy can reduce our expectation of seeing people powerfully touched by Jesus (because, after all, it is the end times), then we have been duped into becoming spectators instead of world-changing participants in life.

CONCLUDING THOUGHTS

In describing the events of the day of Pentecost, Peter says, "But this is what was spoken by the prophet Joel: 'And it shall come to pass in the last days,' says God, 'That I will pour out of My Spirit on all flesh'" (Acts 2:16-18). Peter says the events of Acts 2 were end-time events. How quickly could we transform the world if, instead of living a lifestyle molded by fear and fatalism, we modeled our end-time attitudes and behaviors after the believers in the book of Acts?

DISCUSSION QUESTIONS

1. What truth stood out to you the most in this teaching?
2. How has end times teaching been a negative and/or positive influence in your life?
3. How do your beliefs about the end times align with God's?

SPEAK THESE DECLARATIONS ALOUD

- God's kingdom will expand mightily in the end times.
- God's promises are true for me regardless of what is happening in the world.
- I have healthy, hope-filled beliefs about the end times.

29 GOD WON'T OVERRIDE SOMEONE'S FREE WILL

CONTEXT

"The Lord is not slack concerning His promise, as some count slackness, but is longsuffering toward us, not willing that any should perish but that all should come to repentance" (2 Peter 3:9). God's heart is for all to be in a right relationship with Him, but He waits for them to make that decision (and does not force them to do so).

POSITIVE

As the verse above indicates, God is longsuffering (patient) toward us. He is a "whosoever" God that gives every person the free choice to choose Him or not. "For God so loved the world that He gave His only begotten Son, that whoever believes in Him should not perish but have everlasting life" (John 3:16). Even though God desires to influence every person toward repentance through the prayers, faith, and obedience of His people, He has not created robots that He has predestined to be one way or another.

CHECKING THE FOUNDATION

There will be a crack in our spiritual foundation if we believe that we are not capable of having a powerful influence on people that would make it difficult for them to reject God's plan for their lives. The power of prayer, faith, love, prophecy, wisdom, impartation, speaking life, and standing on the promises of God are mighty weapons that can free those who have been blinded (2 Corinthians 4:4). Once the blinders have been removed and God is seen as He really is, it would be a hard thing indeed for a person to reject our Savior. This person's free will has not been overridden, but it has been influenced greatly in the right direction.

CONCLUDING THOUGHTS

Does a dog have a free will if a piece of steak is placed in front of his nose? In one sense the answer is yes; but in a greater sense, the answer is a definite no. In a similar way, we have the awesome privilege to put the true Jesus in front of people. We must be diligent in using our spiritual gifts for others and not become passive because of a "God does not override a person's free will" teaching. Let us never doubt that we have within us everything necessary to radically influence people towards making their decision for Jesus Christ.

DISCUSSION QUESTIONS

1. What truth stood out to you the most in this teaching?
2. How much do you believe you can radically influence people?
3. What specific steps can you take to cause people to come to Christ and/or to have great breakthrough in Him?

SPEAK THESE DECLARATIONS ALOUD

- People around me want to get saved.
- I dramatically influence people to walk in their true identity.
- I am an influencer of influencers.

30 ALL WHO DESIRE TO LIVE GODLY WILL SUFFER PERSECUTION

CONTEXT

Paul writes to his spiritual son, Timothy, "But you have carefully followed my doctrine, manner of life, purpose, faith, longsuffering, love, perseverance, persecutions, afflictions, which happened to me at Antioch, at Iconium, at Lystra – what persecutions I endured. And out of them all the Lord delivered me. Yes, and all who desire to live godly in Christ Jesus will suffer persecution" (2 Timothy 2:1-12).

POSITIVE

All Christians need to have a willingness to be mistreated (and even die if necessary) for their faith in Jesus. Those who are on the front lines of bringing Christ to godless and demonically ruled cultures may especially face challenging situations. Paul is an example of someone who endured suffering for Christ, but he also declared God's great deliverance for him out of these persecutions.

CHECKING THE FOUNDATION

There will be a crack in our spiritual foundation if we believe that we will be disliked because we are Christian. It is unwise to believe that non-Christians (or even church people) will reject us. It is better to have faith that the force of favor will cause us to prosper in all situations, even in very godless places (consider Daniel and Joseph). Favor will cause people to have a desire to cooperate with us. 1 Timothy 2:1-3 exhorts us to pray and give thanks "...that we may lead a quiet and peaceable life in all godliness and reverence. For this is good and acceptable in the sight of God our Savior." Jesus also "increased... in favor with God and men" (Luke 2:52). Even though Christ's end purpose was a sacrificial death for us, we realize that increasing favor was a key to His life (and so it is to be with us).

CONCLUDING THOUGHTS

It is foolish for us to expect poor relationships with people. While martyrdom and mistreatment are a reality for the body of Christ (especially in some areas of the world), some believers have mistaken a result of poor people skills and lack of wisdom as "persecution." It is important to understand that the expectation of favor or the expectation of persecution can attract either to our lives. We would do well to expect the force of favor to open many doors to us for the kingdom's sake.

DISCUSSION QUESTIONS

1. What truth stood out to you the most in this teaching?
2. Do you believe Christians should expect favor in the eyes of non-Christians? Why or why not?
3. How do you believe the kingdom advancing will affect crime, family dynamics, addictive behaviors, and the amount of blessing we walk in? Please explain.

SPEAK THESE DECLARATIONS ALOUD

- The force of favor in my life causes me to prosper in all situations.
- My favor is increasing with God and man.
- I have great people skills, and I walk in wisdom in all my relationships.

31 THE ANOINTING OF GOD SETS PEOPLE FREE

CONTEXT

Jesus said in John 20:21, "As the Father has sent Me, so I send you." In Luke 4:18 Jesus describes how the Father sent Him: "The Spirit of the Lord is upon Me because He has anointed Me to preach the gospel to the poor; He has sent Me to heal the brokenhearted, to proclaim liberty to the captives and recovery of sight to the blind, to set at liberty those who are oppressed." Acts 10:38 confirms this, "How God anointed Jesus... with the Holy Spirit and with power, who went about doing good and healing all who were oppressed by the devil, for God was with Him."

POSITIVE

Jesus claimed that the anointing of the Spirit on His life was the key to setting people free from bondage, emotional difficulties, spiritual blindness, and poverty. When He was baptized in the Spirit, He became anointed to do what He could not do in the first thirty years of His life. We too are called to receive by faith an infusion of power (an anointing) to set people free – for one encounter with the anointing of God can change a life forever.

CHECKING THE FOUNDATION

There will be a crack in our spiritual foundation if we believe that the devil is primarily resisted and defeated by a Spirit encounter instead of a truth revelation. The power of God does wonderfully set people free, but staying free comes from believing truth instead of lies. In the long run, it isn't the beliefs of the one praying for me that matters most, but it is my own beliefs that will set the course of my life. Jesus defeated the devil in the wilderness by speaking truth that He believed (see Matthew 4:1-11). Our Lord powerfully reinforced this in John 8:31-32: "If you abide in my word, you are My disciples indeed; and you will know the truth and the truth will set you free."

CONCLUDING THOUGHTS

We need a greater demonstration of the anointing of God in our lives and our ministries. We must pursue its manifestation with relentless tenacity. However, we must avoid the tendency to depend on the anointing of "super Christians" and special meetings to make us free instead of knowing the truth about God, our circumstances, our past, our future, and ourselves.

DISCUSSION QUESTIONS

1. What truth stood out to you the most in this teaching?
2. What role does the Holy Spirit have in our freedom, and what role does truth have in it?
3. What can we learn from Jesus in how He withstood the devil in Matthew 4?

SPEAK THESE DECLARATIONS ALOUD

- I carry a breaker anointing to bring people into greater levels of freedom.
- I am a person of the Word, and I am a person of the Spirit.
- Because I abide in the Word, I know the truth, and the truth makes me free.

32 NO MAN CAN CONTROL THE TONGUE

CONTEXT

"For every kind of beast and bird, of reptile and creature of the sea, is tamed and has been tamed by mankind. But no man can tame the tongue. It is an unruly evil, full of deadly poison. With it we bless our God and Father, and with it we curse men who have been made in the similitude of God" (James 3:7-9).

POSITIVE

It is the nature of unredeemed people to gravitate toward sinful choices, and this certainly includes saying destructive words in the form of gossip, cussing, angry outbursts, criticism, self-pronounced curses, lying, slander, and general negativity. But we have been redeemed through Christ and are new creations (2 Corinthians 5:17), and we can do all things (including controlling our tongues) through Christ who strengthens us (Philippians 4:13).

CHECKING THE FOUNDATION

There will be a crack in our spiritual foundation if we think that we are destined to (and should expect) negative speech in our lives, in our families, and in our churches. Instead, we see hope in verses such as Ephesians 4:29, "Let no corrupt words proceed out your mouth" (because we understand that we will never be commanded to do something we cannot do). This truth goes far beyond stopping the negative talk; but more importantly, it teaches us the powerful principle of speaking life as a positive force in all aspects of life. "The power of life and death is in the tongue, and those who love it will eat the fruit of it" (Proverbs 18:21). "Those who love it" are those who proactively, enthusiastically, and joyfully use words to plant seeds for their future. (They "plant" words that will bring great fruit to "eat" in relationships, health, ministry, vocation, finances, protection, and overall blessing.)

CONCLUDING THOUGHTS

We must be vigilant to put a guard over our mouths so that we don't curse others and ourselves, but there is a higher goal than this. Truly, our tongues can be controlled if we allow the Holy Spirit to lead us and impregnate us with vision, and empower us to the point where we declare with passion, "I love it! I have another opportunity today through my words to impart grace to others, to sow abundant life into my future, and to speak of the wonderful works of God!"

DISCUSSION QUESTIONS

1. What truth stood out to you the most in this teaching?
2. What are ways to increase your revelation about the power of your words?
3. What are the most important situations for you to speak life into?

SPEAK THESE DECLARATIONS ALOUD

- My words impart grace to everyone who hears them.
- The words I speak change lives, families, churches, regions, and nations.
- I am continually increasing the amount of life I produce with my words.

33 WE DON'T NEED TO ATTEND CHURCH TO BE A CHRISTIAN

CONTEXT

This is not a biblical verse, but a phrase that is said by some Christians. In our discussion here, it is understood that the church is a place where people gather regularly to worship God and to spend time with like-minded people.

POSITIVE

It is very true that we don't have to belong to an organized church to be a Christian. We receive eternal life through faith in Christ, not by attending or joining a church. As individuals, we are able to have wonderful fellowship and experiences with God through personal prayer, Bible reading, helping others, soaking, and through contact with other Christians.

CHECKING THE FOUNDATION

There will be a crack in our spiritual foundation if we undervalue the role the church has in our lives. Here are five reasons the church is important: 1) By connecting us regularly with people who honor God and the Bible, church provides positive peer pressure to live victoriously (1 John 1:7). 2) It allows us to use our God-given gifts while being joined with other parts of the body of Christ as described in 1 Corinthians 12 and Ephesians 4:15-16. 3) We can be equipped and trained by anointed leadership for our purpose in life (Ephesians 4:11-16). 4) The committed relationships in a church cause us to "grow up" and become consistent in our Christianity – just as marriage and other family covenants cause us to mature. 5) Church provides an exponential increase of our potential to change the world when we join others with our talents, prayers, finances, and fulfilling our "Great Commission" of reaching the world for Christ (Matthew 28:18-20).

CONCLUDING THOUGHTS

There may be situations where we are unable to find a local church to be involved with, and there may be seasons of our lives where our participation is less because of a specific thing that God is doing in us, but we must be careful of trying to live apart from a consistent connection to God's people. Successful living requires a clear order of personal priorities. God needs to be #1 and it is clear from Scripture (and from life experience) that if we don't consistently prioritize Him in our daily life and include prayer, Bible reading, fellowship, and worship in our schedules, we will have difficulty truly living for God.

DISCUSSION QUESTIONS

1. What truth stood out to you the most in this teaching?
2. Why is it important for Christians to fellowship regularly with a specific group of believers?
3. What group of people has God called you to? How do you live out your role in the body?

SPEAK THESE DECLARATIONS ALOUD

- I am a vital, functioning part of a fellowship of believers.
- I have strong priorities in my life, and one of my greatest priorities involves my commitment to a specific group of people.
- Whatever changes need to happen in the church are happening.

34 IT'S NOT ABOUT ME

CONTEXT

"Let nothing be done through selfish ambition or conceit, but in lowliness of mind let each esteem others better than himself. Let each of you look out not only for his own interests, but also for the interests of others. Let this mind be in you which was also in Christ Jesus, who... made Himself of no reputation, taking the form of a bondservant ..." (Philippians 2:3-7).

POSITIVE

Jesus has a way of delivering us from selfishness and self-centeredness. He calls us to get our eyes off of ourselves, and put our sight on Him and the needs of other people. He has delivered us from self-reliance, self-justifying behavior, self-righteousness, self-preservation, self-pity, self-promotion, and self-protection; and He has made a way for us to stay free from them.

CHECKING THE FOUNDATION

There will be a crack in our spiritual foundation if, in our zeal to be selfless, we don't have a clear plan to stay healthy physically, emotionally, spiritually, financially, mentally, and relationally. What good is it if we help people now, but experience burnout early in life because we failed to understand basic wisdom and priorities for successful living? Also, those who are constantly taking care of the "needs" of others are often enabling those people to be increasingly irresponsible and dependent on them. Finally, it is necessary to guard against using our zealous serving and "selfless Christianity" as an escape or justification for why we don't get help in our own lives for major unresolved personal issues and/or family dysfunction.

CONCLUDING THOUGHTS

It is truly "not about me." As Jesus did, I must "lay my life down" for the people in my life. We do, however, need to understand that this self-sacrifice is not always about meeting the immediate needs and wants of others. Laying our lives down is also a commitment to personal increase so we can meet more needs and prepare ourselves to be able to give much more in the future. It is important to have healthy boundaries in place, so we can stay healthy and have longevity.

DISCUSSION QUESTIONS

1. What truth stood out to you the most in this teaching?
2. How can you improve your plan to stay healthy in life, while still refraining from being selfish?
3. Successful people prioritize the important, but not urgent, aspects of life. How would you assess your own tendencies regarding this? Please explain.

SPEAK THESE DECLARATIONS ALOUD

- My life purpose is not about my happiness, but it is to know God and to make Him known.
- I am not only responding to the urgent demands around me, I am regularly investing in the important areas of life.
- I have a great plan to stay healthy physically, emotionally, spiritually, mentally, and relationally.

35 LET ALL THINGS BE DONE DECENTLY AND IN ORDER

CONTEXT

In 1 Corinthians chapter 14, the Apostle Paul explains the purpose of prophecy and tongues in the church, and he gives guidelines for their use. In concluding his teaching on this, he writes, "Therefore, brethren, desire earnestly to prophesy, and do not forbid to speak with tongues. Let all things be done decently and in order" (1 Corinthians 14:40).

POSITIVE

The Corinthian church seemed to be a "free for all" in their use (or abuse) of spiritual gifts. Apparently, their meetings were dominated with lengthy messages in tongues. Paul painstakingly gave direction and order for the proper use of tongues and spiritual gifts. He strongly encourages their use, but provides boundaries for using them in beneficial ways. Church leaders today also need to guide and direct the operation of spiritual gifts so that things are done "decently and in order" for people to be consistently blessed under their leadership.

CHECKING THE FOUNDATION

There will be a crack in our spiritual foundation if we think that "decent and in order" means that nothing potentially odd or discomforting will happen in our church meetings. We need to realize that wherever there is new life, there will be great potential for "messes." Wherever there is true spiritual fire, there will be some "wild fire" happening that seems out of control. Cemeteries are "decent and in order," but there is no life there. Many churches are so decent and in order that God encounters are rare or non-existent.

CONCLUDING THOUGHTS

We need to pray for church leaders as they seek to lead their ministries with wisdom concerning the moving of the Holy Spirit. On the one hand, they must establish order, structure, and boundaries concerning the operation and manifestation of the Holy Spirit in meetings. On the other hand, leaders need to create a "wineskin" where there is a freedom to experience God powerfully and spontaneously in ways that some would say is not decent and in order. This wineskin is made up of ingredients like: 1) encouraging Christ-centered risk taking, 2) training in the gifts of the Spirit, 3) empowering and trusting people to minister in the "anointing," 4) having strong accountability, 5) valuing joy, 6) not overly planning meetings, and 7) esteeming passionate worship. This wineskin may not bring about safe predictability, but the results will be "decent and in order" in God's eyes.

DISCUSSION QUESTIONS

1. What truth stood out to you the most in this teaching?
2. What is the balance between having freedom in meetings but still having leadership direct what is happening? What are the signs of too much "freedom" and the signs of too much control?
3. What can you do to increase the likelihood of Holy Spirit encounters in your life?

SPEAK THESE DECLARATIONS ALOUD

- I walk in great wisdom concerning the move of the Holy Spirit in me and through me.
- I regularly have powerful encounters with God.
- I lead meetings like those experienced in the Book of Acts.

36 GOD HELPS THOSE WHO HELP THEMSELVES

CONTEXT

This phrase is an ancient proverb that shows up in the literature of many cultures, including a 1736 edition of Benjamin Franklin's Poor Richard's Almanac. However, it does not appear in the Bible.

POSITIVE

The Bible has many promises that depend on us doing our part. Examples are: 1) "If we call on His name, we will be saved" (Romans 10:13). 2) "If we draw near to Him, He will draw near to us" (James 4:8). 3) "If we sow to the Spirit, we will reap life" (Galatians 6:8). 4) "If we pray, He will answer" (Matthew 7:7). 5) "If we forgive, we will be forgiven" (Matthew 6:14). 6) "If we sow bountifully, we will reap bountifully" (2 Corinthians 9:6). Indeed, there are many ways that God seemingly "helps" those who are seeking Him, honoring His spiritual laws, and are devoted to serving Him.

CHECKING THE FOUNDATION

There will be a crack in our spiritual foundation if we believe that God is more concerned with what we do than what we believe. Certainly good works are important, but they are not what save us or what primarily move the hand of God in our lives. Consider Ephesians 2:8-9 – "For by grace you have been saved through faith, and that not of yourselves; it is the gift of God, not of works, lest anyone should boast." Galatians 3:2-5 takes this further – "This only I want to learn from you: Did you receive the Spirit by the works of the law, or by the hearing of faith? Are you so foolish? Having begun in the Spirit, are you now being made perfect by the flesh?... Therefore He who supplies the Spirit to you and works miracles among you, does He do it by the works of the law, or by the hearing of faith?" It is obvious that God ultimately "helps" those who believe and have faith, not those who think their moral superiority (works of the law) attracts God's blessing.

CONCLUDING THOUGHTS

Hard work is a great quality, but God is not looking to help those who help themselves. He is looking for those who will have a radical belief in His Son and in His Word (the Bible), which will release a supernatural, divine empowerment that "helps" them do what they never thought they could do.

DISCUSSION QUESTIONS

1. What truth stood out to you the most in this teaching?
2. What are ways to move from being conduct focused to being beliefs focused in your life?
3. Why do some Christians seem to be focused on keeping rules rather than building a relationship fueled by healthy beliefs?

SPEAK THESE DECLARATIONS ALOUD

- I am diligent and hard working in the important things of my life.
- My belief in God releases a continual flow of supernatural grace to me.
- I am not only saved by grace through faith, but I also grow and advance in my Christian walk by grace through faith.

37 BEING SINCERE IS THE MOST IMPORTANT THING

CONTEXT

This phrase is never directly quoted in Scripture, but we are instructed in many places in the Bible to be pure in heart, to be sincere, and to have good motives in what we do.

POSITIVE

Two definitions for sincere are: 1) honest and unaffected in a way that shows what is said is really meant; and 2) based on what is truly and deeply felt. These are qualities that are essential for being an effective Christian. In addition to this, the word "good" means to "have or show an upright and virtuous character." These qualities are vital for our lives. It is absolutely necessary that we go after having a good heart which possesses patience, kindness, loyalty, honesty, genuine care for others, and which esteems integrity and honor in relationships over our desire for money or position in life.

CHECKING THE FOUNDATION

There will be a crack in our spiritual foundation if we believe that sincerity and kindness override negative beliefs and poor personal priorities. There are many sincere people who are sincerely wrong. There are numerous Christians who have good hearts, but are still imprisoned in a "wilderness Christianity." John the Baptist and Jesus did not say, "Be sincere, for the kingdom of God is at hand!" No – they said, "Repent, for the kingdom of God is at hand" (Matthew 3:2). Repentance is changing the way we think so that we believe God's promises instead of lies. Unless we continually renew our minds (Romans 12:2), we will not have lasting breakthrough, even if we have a good heart. Repentance also involves doing things God's way and not our own way. Wrong choices, even with a good heart, can cause great problems.

CONCLUDING THOUGHTS

Every Christian needs to move towards having a sincere heart and good motives in all that is done. Without this, we are headed for a shipwreck in our lives. Even so, we also need to recognize that these great qualities are not enough to defeat the devil in our lives or see the kingdom advance through us.

DISCUSSION QUESTIONS

1. What truth stood out to you the most in this teaching?
2. What are some keys to growing in sincerity in your walk with the Lord?
3. How have you upgraded your thinking (repented) in a key area of your life?

SPEAK THESE DECLARATIONS ALOUD

- I am diligent and work hard in the important things of my life.
- My beliefs in God release a continual flow of supernatural grace to me.
- I am growing in compassion towards others.

38 PEOPLE CLOSE TO GOD STRUGGLE IN RELATIONSHIPS

CONTEXT

This is not a Bible verse but is the belief and experience of some.

POSITIVE

Those who "shut themselves in with God" can seem out of step with what is going on in the lives of most people. Godly people have higher standards in decision making and life choices, and this can be unpopular in society. Church attendees who know about God and have yet to build intimacy with Him sometimes criticize passionate saints; thus, there can be a strain in relationships. God will give us wisdom if we ask Him (James 1:5), and wisdom knows how to communicate and do relationships well.

CHECKING THE FOUNDATION

There will be a crack in our spiritual foundation if we believe that continued strained relationships are a sign of our closeness to God (or a sign that people are rejecting something righteous in us). People problems are often an indication of our immaturity. Consider this: if we are only respected and liked by those who have spent little time with us, then we probably have a character problem that needs to be addressed. Too often, misunderstandings and problems in relationships come from violating basic "relationship protocols" (such as being ungrateful, irritable, undependable, tactless in speech, rude, poor at listening, a slanderer of people, dishonoring and hurtful to immediate family members, and irresponsible for past relationship "messes" that need to be cleaned up).

CONCLUDING THOUGHTS

We don't want to compromise to be acceptable to lukewarm Christians and non-believers, but we certainly don't want to use rejection as a badge of honor to prove we are close to God. We must be careful that we don't justify relationship breakdowns and then focus on the faults of those seemingly against us. It is the wise person who gets to the root of his or her relational problems so that there can be true respect from family members, close associates, and others. Not everyone may like us, but if people don't respect us, then we may have work to do in cleaning up past "messes" in our relationships.

DISCUSSION QUESTIONS

1. What truth stood out to you the most in this teaching?
2. What are some of the reasons that people close to God can be misunderstood?
3. What are steps to take to improve the relationships in our lives?

SPEAK THESE DECLARATIONS ALOUD

- I have healthy long-term relationships.
- I am passionate about my relationship with the Lord and my relationships with other people.
- I am well respected by my peers.

39 EVERY BRANCH THAT BEARS FRUIT HE PRUNES

CONTEXT

"I am the true vine, and My Father is the vinedresser. Every branch in Me that does not bear fruit He takes away; and every branch that bears fruit He prunes, that it may bear more fruit. You are already clean because of the word which I have spoken to you. Abide in Me, and I in you. As the branch cannot bear fruit of itself, unless it abides in the vine, neither can you, unless you abide in Me" (John 15:1-4).

POSITIVE

Plants need to be pruned for a variety of reasons. Pruning allows them to be shaped to desirable sizes and characteristics to compliment the rest of a garden or yard. Also, pruning removes dead, diseased, or damaged branches or stems. This increases the overall well-being and beauty of vegetation. God also prunes our lives of old thought patterns and old behaviors that will hinder us from bearing greater fruit in the days ahead.

CHECKING THE FOUNDATION

There will be a crack in our spiritual foundation if we believe that God prunes us primarily through negative circumstances, rather than by "cutting back" old belief patterns in our lives. We must understand that it is not our actions that are our biggest problem, but it is the way we think. We cannot go to a higher level in our lives without first going to a higher level in what we believe. The reason we are not bearing more fruit now is because there are still strongholds of "dead beliefs" that must be pruned back so we can bear more fruit.

CONCLUDING THOUGHTS

God is pruning each of us for a higher purpose. There may be difficult circumstances involved in this process, but the goal is something much higher than just strengthening our character and perseverance. Our heavenly Gardener is ready to snip off the lies we have believed that have restricted our lives. Let's help Him do it by declaring war once more on our real enemy – which are the falsehoods in our thinking that rob us of faith, hope, and love in our lives, towards others, and about our future.

DISCUSSION QUESTIONS

1. What truth stood out to you the most in this teaching?
2. How are our beliefs connected to moving to higher levels?
3. Do you have any "dead beliefs" that need to be pruned back? What fruit will be the result?

SPEAK THESE DECLARATIONS ALOUD

- God is upgrading my beliefs.
- I am well equipped for my future.
- My new belief patterns are creating greater fruit in my life.

40 GOD WANTS YOU TO DIE

CONTEXT

This phrase is not in the Bible, but is sometimes used in messages and books to describe the dying to self-will that must happen in a Christian's life. It is presented often like this: "We ask Jesus in our hearts; and we expect to be blessed, but we find out that God really wants to kill us."

POSITIVE

We cannot simply add Jesus to our own plans, priorities, and ways of doing things. We have to "die" to "doing our own thing" and live for His purposes and plans for us. Our old responses and thinking patterns are to be put on "death row." This can be somewhat surprising (and at times painful). Like a drug addict who is going "cold turkey," we can experience withdrawals from our old thinking patterns that seem to be killing us. However, as we persevere and continue to renew our minds with truth, our lives will be transformed (Romans 12:2).

CHECKING THE FOUNDATION

There will be a crack in our spiritual foundation if we believe that God desires to bring us into constant hard times to mature us. This doctrinal belief will actually attract more difficulty. Those who think that God makes our lives miserable to help us grow would need to report Him to the authorities for child abuse. Also, God does not want to kill our uniqueness and creativity. We are not to be robots, but to walk in uniqueness and creativity.

CONCLUDING THOUGHTS

Religion presents God as a killjoy, and we must be careful that we don't reinforce this by overemphasizing dying to self and underemphasizing celebrating Christ's death for us. The war against our flesh is primarily won by "hiding God's Word in our hearts that we might not sin against Him" (Psalm 119:11) and knowing as we live and walk in the Spirit, the fruit of the Spirit will grow in our lives (Galatians 5:16).

DISCUSSION QUESTIONS

1. What truth stood out to you the most in this teaching?
2. What does it mean to die to self?
3. How does God want to mature us and continually develop our uniqueness and creativity?

SPEAK THESE DECLARATIONS ALOUD

- I have the mind of Christ.
- Jesus is the focus of my plans, my priorities, and my way of doing things.
- God celebrates my uniqueness and creativity.

41 THIS KIND COMES OUT ONLY BY PRAYER AND FASTING

CONTEXT

The story in Mark 9 is about a boy who has a demon. Jesus' disciples tried to cast it out and could not. When Jesus discovered that they failed, He puts the blame on a lack of faith ("O faithless generation..."). Later in the same chapter He says, "This kind comes out only by prayer and fasting" (Mark 9:29).

POSITIVE

Fasting (the abstaining of food or certain types of food) is a discipline, spiritual law, and spiritual weapon that is mentioned frequently in the Old and New Testaments. It is powerful help for our own spiritual growth and for "breakthrough praying." A lifestyle of prayer and fasting increases intimacy with God and spiritual power.

CHECKING THE FOUNDATION

There will be a crack in our spiritual foundation if we conclude any of the following: 1) God responds to my works instead of my faith. 2) Fasting is necessary to see my sinful habits crucified. 3) God's hand moves to the degree that I am willing to suffer and deny myself. 4) Demons won't leave unless I have a "worthiness" based on recent self-sacrifice and spiritual consistency.

CONCLUDING THOUGHTS

Fasting and faith are important, but faith is the key. Faith (not works) moves mountains. Good works (whether fasting or anything else) do not convince God to act on our behalf. Galatians 3:5 states that miracles and the "supply of the Spirit" come by faith, not by works of the law. Fasting has its place in helping produce faith, but by itself, it does not increase the likelihood of God responding to us. Demons flee from those who are secure in Christ. Our faith (or lack thereof) is the deciding factor in whether or not evil is evicted in our areas of responsibility and authority. Fasting can help us to move from "faith-empty" to "faith-full."

DISCUSSION QUESTIONS

1. What truth stood out to you the most in this teaching?
2. How is fasting spiritual warfare?
3. How does fasting increase intimacy with God and spiritual power?

SPEAK THESE DECLARATIONS ALOUD

- My faith moves mountains.
- My security in God is a threat to the enemy.
- When I pray and fast I am increasing my intimacy with God and spiritual power. FAST to DRAW NEAR

FASTING increases MY INTIMACY w/ GOD AND CHANGES ME FROM

(FAITH-empts) to FaithFull)

42 PARTIAL OBEDIENCE IS NOT OBEDIENCE

CONTEXT

This is not a phrase in Scripture, but it is a truth that is illustrated in 1 Samuel 15 where King Saul did not fully obey the command by Samuel concerning the Amalakites and King Agag. Saul was sharply rebuked for this and ultimately lost his kingdom because of a root of double-mindedness and half-hearted obedience.

POSITIVE

It is vital for Christians to follow through on the voice of the Lord in their lives. It is too easy to start something and then finish in an incomplete manner. The second seed of the Parable of the Sower (Mark 4) gives insight on this. That seed fell on shallow ground. This represents those who lose interest when the excitement wears off. This shallowness of commitment and follow-through is a huge issue for us and is to be resisted just as much as any other sin. We must build the internal "muscle" of finishing what we start. David "finished off" Goliath by cutting his head off. We too are to go against our feelings (often tiredness or complacency) and do what God has said.

CHECKING THE FOUNDATION

There will be a crack in our spiritual foundation if we believe that outward success is the measure of true obedience. Just as a baby learns to walk, we too must learn how to obey God in many areas of our lives. When we seem to fail in attempting to live at a higher level of Christianity, we need to realize that "falling down" often precedes "walking" consistently.

CONCLUDING THOUGHTS

(PETER walking /sinKing ON THE WATER.)

Learning to follow through on what God has spoken to us is important. It is also vital to understand that as we grow in God, we will make mistakes in learning to truly follow the Lord's leading. (Remember Peter, who stepped out of the boat onto the water with his eyes on Jesus, but began to sink when he took his eyes off of his Savior?) Like Peter, those who seek to obey what the Lord is saying will appear to fail more than those who are "playing it safe" from inside the boat. Let's not become condemned when we seemingly fail as we step out of the boat of past comforts and familiar ways of doing things. More importantly, let's not revert back to a comfortable and "failure-proof" Christianity that settles for mediocrity and non-accountability for what God has told us to do.

DISCUSSION QUESTIONS

1. What truth stood out to you the most in this teaching?
2. What does successful obedience look like?
3. Why will those who seek to obey appear to fail more?

SPEAK THESE DECLARATIONS ALOUD

- I always follow through on what God is asking me to do.
- I am learning to walk consistently with the Holy Spirit.
- I walk in increasing excellence and accountability as I follow what God has called me to do.

RISK and GROWTH are CONNECTED

- I WILL MAKE MISTAKES AS I LEARN TO FOLLOW GOD's VOICE
- ITS OKAY. A BABY LEARNS FROM FALLING, FAILING → THEN BREAKTHROUGH

43 CALLING THINGS THAT ARE NOT AS THOUGH THEY ARE

CONTEXT

"As it is written, "I have made you a father of many nations", in the presence of Him whom he believed – God, who gives life to the dead and calls those things which do not exist as though they did" (Romans 4:17). In this verse, God reveals His strategy for bringing life to dead situations – which is "naming and calling" things by His promises instead of what they seem to be. Abram is used as an example of this truth. His miracle promise was made manifest after he called himself Abraham (which means "father of a multitude").

POSITIVE

"Faith comes by hearing and hearing by the Word of God" (Romans 10:17). Our speaking of God's promises not only affects the spiritual atmosphere, but more importantly, builds up (edifies) our belief system to truly believe who God says we are and who He says He is. Joel says, "Let the weak say I am strong" (Joel 3:10). Calling ourselves by the promises of God is a key for breakthrough for our lives. As long as we call ourselves by our past experiences, we are locked into repeating them.

CHECKING THE FOUNDATION

There will be a crack in our spiritual foundation if we think that this verse says the opposite of what it really says. It does not say, "Calling those things that are as though they are not." To do this would be living in denial. The Bible does not teach us to say, "I am not sick, or I am not weak in that area." That would be a lie and focusing on the negative, rather than concentrating on God's solutions. Some, in the name of faith, have thought that denying the negative is the key to seeing it leave. In reality, the presence of the positive is what evicts the negative. Remember, the best way to get rid of darkness is to turn on the light.

CONCLUDING THOUGHTS

Christians don't deny the facts of current situations. We are called to address these with responsibility and wisdom. We do, however, choose to focus more on God's truths and promises rather than just the facts of what is currently happening. Like Abraham, we are called to declare the great, laughable promises over our lives, even when all circumstances are screaming, "It will never happen!"

DISCUSSION QUESTIONS

1. What truth stood out to you the most in this teaching?
2. What is God's strategy for bringing life to dead situations?
3. Explain the difference between "calling those things which do not exist as though they did" and denial?

SPEAK THESE DECLARATIONS ALOUD

- I increasingly walk in truth, responsibility, and wisdom.
- By calling myself by the promises of God, I am attracting breakthrough to my life.
- I choose to focus more on the truth of God's promises than the facts of what is happening.

No DENIAL!
CONGRUENT
essential!

THE BELIEVER'S TRUTH
1. ACKNOWLEDGE REALITY of CIRCUMSTANCE
2. PROCLAIM the KINGDOM PROMISE
3. TURN on THE LIGHT
   and DARKNESS FLEES.

ADDITIONAL RESOURCES

VICTORIOUS MINDSETS

What we believe is ultimately more important than what we do. The course of our lives is set by our deepest core beliefs. Our mindsets are either a stronghold for God's purposes or a playhouse for the enemy. In this book, fifty biblical attitudes are revealed that are foundational for those who desire to walk in freedom and power.

HELP! I'M A PASTOR

Help! I'm a Pastor addresses many common situations in church life that few seem really prepared for. It gives tools to successfully addressing these happenings with humor, healthy beliefs, and divine strategies. The truths presented will help every church leader become more proactive in his or her leadership, plus be able to equip their teams with the core values necessary to create healthy ministries. This book includes 80 life and leadership core values and 50 scenarios.

YOU'RE CRAZY IF YOU DON'T TALK TO YOURSELF

Jesus did not just think His way out of the wilderness and neither can we. He spoke truth to invisible beings and mindsets that sought to restrict and defeat Him. This book reveals that life and death are truly in the power of the tongue, and emphasizes the necessity of speaking truth to our souls. Our words really do set the course of our lives and the lives of others (Proverbs 18:21, James 3:2-5).

ADDITIONAL RESOURCES

LIVING FROM THE UNSEEN

This book will help you identify beliefs that block the reception of God's blessings and hinder our ability to live out our destiny. This book reveals that: 1) Believing differently, not trying harder, is the key to change, 2) You cannot do what you don't believe you are, 3) You can only receive what you think you are worth, 4) Rather than learning how to die – it is time to learn how to live.

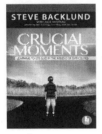

CRUCIAL MOMENTS

This book helps us upgrade how we think, act, and most importantly, believe in crucial moments such as: 1) you feel nervous about speaking in public, 2) your house is a mess when people come over, 3) a politician whose beliefs oppose yours is elected, 4) you gain more weight than you thought, 5) you don't feel like worshiping, and 47 other opportunities for breakthrough.

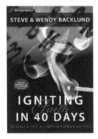

IGNITING FAITH IN 40 DAYS

There must be special seasons in our lives when we break out of routine and do something that will ignite our faith about God and our identity in Christ. This book will lead you through the life-changing experience of a 40-day negativity fast. This fast teaches the power of declaring truth and other transforming daily customs that will strengthen your foundation of faith and radically increase your personal hope.

ADDITIONAL RESOURCES

DIVINE STRATEGIES FOR INCREASE

The laws of the spirit are more real than the natural laws. God's laws are primarily principles to release blessing, not rules to be obeyed to gain right standing with God. The Psalmist talks of one whose greatest delight is in the law of the Lord. This delight allows one to discover new aspects of the nature of God (hidden in each law) to behold and worship. The end result of this delighting is a transformed life that prospers in every endeavor. His experience can be our experience, and this book unlocks the blessings hidden in the spiritual realm.

POSSESSING JOY

In His presence is fullness of joy (Psalm 16:11). Joy is to increase as we go deeper in our relationship with God. Religious tradition has devalued the role that gladness and laughter have for personal victory and kingdom advancement. His presence may not always produce joy, but if we never or rarely have fullness of joy, we must reevaluate our concept of God. This book takes one on a journey toward the headwaters of the full joy that Jesus often spoke of. Get ready for joy to increase and strength and longevity to ignite.

DECLARATIONS

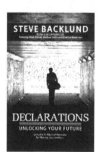

"Nothing happens in the kingdom unless a declaration is made." Believers everywhere are realizing the power of declarations to empower their lives. You may be wondering, "What are declarations and why are people making them?" or maybe, "Aren't declarations simply a repackaged 'name it and claim it' heresy?" *Declarations* answers these questions by sharing 30 biblical reasons for declaring truth over every area of life. Steve Backlund and his team also answer common objections and concerns to the teaching about declarations. The revelation this book carries will help you to set the direction your life will go. Get ready for 30 days of powerful devotions and declarations that will convince you that life is truly in the power of the tongue.

ADDITIONAL RESOURCES

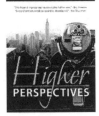

HIGHER PERSPECTIVES
God sees things from a higher perspective. In the Bible, we see many individuals that walked in a revelation of His point of view. Numbers 13 illustrates this when it tells the story of the twelve men sent to spy out the Promised Land. Ten come back with a "realistic" perspective of defeat and victimhood, while Joshua and Caleb come back seeing from God's higher perspective and proclaim, "Let us go up at once. We are well able to overcome it!" Isn't it fascinating that two groups of people can see the same set of circumstances but put different conclusions based on their perspectives? This is a book that studies the incredible, life-altering beliefs of some of our favorite Bible characters. Their supernatural perspective is an invitation for us to see and live as they did.

LET'S JUST LAUGH AT THAT
Our hope level is an indicator of whether we are believing truth or lies. Truth creates hope and freedom, but believing lies brings hopelessness and restriction. We can have great theology but still be powerless because of deception about the key issues of life. Many of these self-defeating mindsets exist in our subconscious and have never been identified. This book exposes numerous falsehoods and reveals truth that makes us free. Get ready for a joy-infused adventure into hope-filled living.

Audio messages are available through the Igniting Hope store at:
IgnitingHope.com
All books are available at shop.ibethel.org
All books available on Kindle at Amazon.com

ABOUNDING HOPE AND JOY

6-part teaching from Steve and Wendy
Available in MP3 and M4V download, CD, and DVD

shop.ibethel.org

You will laugh, be filled with hope, and get tools for victorious living!

IGNITING HOPE MINISTRIES

ignitinghope.com

SELECTED EXCERPTS:

SCENARIO

Pastor Ernie M. Powerment has developed a team of leaders to help him lead and to share in the preaching ministry. Recently Ronny Revelator shared a message based on a book he is reading entitled, *Annihilating Sacred Cows in the Church*. Ernie thinks some of what Ronny said was unscriptural. While Ernie believes we will continually see new things in Scripture to be taught, he now realizes some of those who teach and preach have never had any formal Bible or theological training. He is concerned about this and the potential for heresy. If you were Ernie, what would you do?

LIES ASSOCIATED WITH THIS SCENARIO

- As long as a person has a good heart and has "been with Jesus," we should not question what he or she preaches.
- If someone is accused of teaching heresy, it is always true.
- Pastors who would have concerns about new revelations must be controlling and have a religious spirit.
- All truth from the Bible has already been revealed, so we should always be suspicious of anything preached that we have not heard before.

LIFE AND LEADERSHIP CORE VALUES TO CONSIDER

5   I equip people with the basic principles of how to interpret the Bible.
3   I build "bridges" in my teachings to help people move into the deeper things of God.
58 I confront people with love and inspire them to grow by reminding them of their destiny.
51 I focus more on heart connections than outward obedience toward those I lead.
65 I recognize that trust for one another in our leadership team is a necessary ingredient for our ministry to go forward.

DISCERNING WHAT GOD IS DEVELOPING IN ME

- I am learning to be vigilant in establishing my ministry as a safe place.
- I have the opportunity to develop good accountability in what we teach as a leadership team.
- I get to become stronger in my biblical doctrine while still being open to fresh perspectives on Scripture.

QUESTIONS TO ASK BEFORE TAKING ACTION

1. What protocols keep us accountable for what we teach and preach?
2. Do I really understand what Ronny is trying to say?
3. Is this a one time thing or a pattern for Ronny?
4. Is my goal to discover truth or seek agreement on my current understanding?
5. Is this really heresy, or am I stuck in a wrong belief?

PRACTICAL STEPS TO CONSIDER

1. **Regularly train teachers and preachers** – One of the main responsibilities of senior leaders is to equip their people to become leaders. Part of this equipping will include training in how to teach and preach. These "preaching classes" give opportunities for people to grow in their overall skill and anointing in sharing God's word. Protocols for proper biblical interpretation should be part of these classes. It is recommended that everyone who preaches and teaches in the church be a part of an annual refresher class including these protocols.

2. **Teach your people how to properly interpret the Bible** – One of the greatest privileges of pastoral leadership is to help people connect personally to God. One main aspect of this assignment is to inspire a love for the Bible and to release strategies for its proper interpretation.

3. **Go after greater revelation but establish safety measures to lessen the chances of wrong doctrine being taught** – Some examples of good safety measures are: a) In order to discuss new revelations being received, develop a group of people to meet with regularly who are hungry for God, believe in the present day power of the Holy Spirit, and who honor the authority of Scripture. b) Take time to live out major doctrinal shifts before dogmatically teaching them. c) When finally sharing these truths, immerse your sermons in Scripture and insert the phrase, "This is what I am not saying..." to avoid misunderstandings in what you are revealing. One final thought – every new revelation from God has been called heretical by someone, so do not be afraid of pursuing fresh understanding from the Bible.

DECLARATIONS

- Our church loves the Bible and has increasing revelation of it.
- Our preachers and teachers have a strong revelatory and biblical foundation for what is taught.
- The five fold office of teacher releases supernatural life in our midst and helps us test what it is being revealed to us.

all things are possible
to him who believes

*"So (Jesus) asked his father, 'How long has this been happening to (your son)?' And he said, 'From childhood. And often he has thrown him both into the fire and into the water to destroy him. But if You can do anything, have compassion on us and help us.' Jesus said to him, 'If you can believe, **all things are possible to him who believes.'** Immediately the father of the child cried out and said with tears, 'Lord, I believe; help my unbelief!"*

Mark 9:21-24

Lower Perspectives

THE BOY'S FATHER COULD HAVE CONCLUDED:

- There were no solutions because of how long this problem existed.

- Jesus got a little carried away in the moment and really meant to say that a few small things are possible if God is in a good mood that day.

- Begging Jesus is more vital than believing in the person of Jesus.

- God is not that concerned about children being emotionally free.

- Jesus was insensitive to focus on his level of faith.

- Declaring "Lord, I believe!" was a lie. His experience proved otherwise.

Elevating Truths

1. **A main key to overcoming obstacles is to develop our beliefs –** The father said to Jesus, "But if You can do anything, have compassion on us and help us." Jesus turned the focus from divine willingness and ability to the father's personal beliefs. Jesus said, "If you can believe, all things are possible to him who believes." The father was invited into a higher perspective that would change everything.

Higher
PERSPECTIVES

2. **The duration of a problem does not determine the likelihood of breakthrough** – The Bible frequently reported the time span of an unresolved difficulty to stir hope in us that long-standing issues have solutions (and are still to be pursued for a miracle). A negative perspective about apparent unmovable situations is a bigger problem than the problem.

3. **Jesus is the author and finisher of our faith** – "Immediately the father of the child cried out and said with tears, 'Lord, I believe; help my unbelief!'" This man of seemingly small faith received a great miracle because of his humility and for "looking unto Jesus, the author and finisher of (his) faith" (Hebrews 12:2). We can do the same.

Giving God Something to Work With

- (**Memorize** Romans 12:2 and John 8:31-32.) *— The Passion Translation*

- **Cry out to God for a revolution** to happen in your beliefs about a long-standing issue.

- **Take a specific step** toward bringing freedom to children and youth.

Declarations to Create Higher Perspectives

Jesus is the author and finisher of my faith.

God has surprising solutions to my long-standing concerns.

My faith brings freedom to my children.

Made in the USA
San Bernardino, CA
12 January 2016